MUSIC BY HEART

Oxford University Press,
*Amen House, London, E.C.*4
GLASGOW NEW YORK TORONTO MELBOURNE WELLINGTON
BOMBAY CALCUTTA MADRAS CAPE TOWN
Geoffrey Cumberlege,
Publisher to the University

MUSIC BY HEART

By LILIAS MACKINNON

'*All complain of want of memory,
but none of want of judgement.*'

DR. THOMAS FULLER
(*Gnomologia*, 1732)

GEOFFREY CUMBERLEGE

OXFORD   UNIVERSITY   PRESS
LONDON   NEW YORK   TORONTO

FIRST PUBLISHED	1938
SECOND IMPRESSION	1941
THIRD IMPRESSION	1944
FOURTH IMPRESSION	1947
FIFTH IMPRESSION	1949

PRINTED IN GREAT BRITAIN BY
MERRITT AND HATCHER, LTD., LONDON, S.E.10.

FOREWORD

VERY humbly I present this book, because my life has been more occupied with music than psychology—a subject profound and at the same time mysterious. But as a child may sometimes see the significance of things unnoticed by a grown person, so have I apparently put my finger on some points concerning the psychology of study, the importance of which has been hitherto neglected in music teaching. The artist finds such things out for himself; but the artist is rarely the best teacher, because, finding things out for himself, he leaves his pupils to do likewise, with the result that many of his most useful ideas remain, for others undeveloped, in the dark-room of his mind.

As a student I was forced to consider memory, because, through having neglected it during many years of sight-reading, I had come to mistrust the parrot memory of my childhood. Undeterred by the prevalence of 'nerves' among my fellow students, I was determined to find some system that would work—a recipe for confidence.

I had before me a big psychological puzzle, and few of the pieces would fit; but after much rearrangement of the many parts, I discovered that I had, not one, but two puzzles to solve, each highly complicated; and that, through a mistake of the teacher in the past, both had been put into the same mental compartment. One of the puzzles was the design of practice; the other the design of performance—subjects so different that I found it difficult to understand how any teacher of intelligence could have mixed them up.

At first I was confused by two portions, one of which was consciousness; the other I discovered to be subconsciousness. The latter I had been led to believe belonged to the puzzle of practice, while the former I tried to fit into my picture of performance.

I had no one to help me, because my fellow students were not interested in psychological puzzles, and the teachers were too busy with examinations; and for years I tried without success to fit subconsciousness into the design of practice. Then one day I had an inspiration, and by changing the pieces I could distinguish the main outlines quite clearly. Consciousness was the centre of practice; subconsciousness the centre of performance. Why had no teacher told me this? The pieces fitted perfectly.

I have continued to work for many years on these two puzzles, and even now I have fitted together but a few of the parts, and there is much to do. But as life is too short to allow me to add many more pieces, I leave it to the psychologist of the future to fill in the most fascinating —the design of the background.

I would offer my sincere thanks to the following experts who have generously given me the benefit of their advice on various parts of the book: Professor Francis Aveling, Sir Adrian Boult, Mr. Basil Cameron, Mr. G. D. Cunningham, Mr. H. Goss Custard, Mr. Alan Frank, Mr. Serge Koussevitzky, Mr. Hans Lange, Dr. Stanley Marchant, C.V.O., and Mr. E. Stanley Roper, M.V.O.

To my correspondence pupils all over the world I am greatly indebted. By sharing with me their problems they have shared their experience, and so we have worked together: it is thanks both to their success and their encouragement that I have been enabled at last to present in book form this outline of Musical Memory.

L. M.

CHELSEA,
April, 1938.

CONTENTS

INTERLUDE

CONTENTS

I

INTRODUCTION—HOW MUSICAL MEMORY DEVELOPED

In the year 1808, during a concert in Leghorn, Paganini had an experience that would have upset most soloists of his day: as soon as he began to play, both the candles fell out of the music desk.

Being accustomed nowadays to see a concert soloist perform 'without the notes', we have to remind ourselves that not until the time of Liszt did playing from memory come into fashion. That musicians were capable of prodigious feats of memory had been proved by the case of Mozart, who wrote down Allegri's *Miserere* at first hearing; but that any one could perform a written work with accuracy and safety 'without book' was at one time considered hardly credible. Indeed, teachers of the past not only discouraged memory-playing, but sternly forbade it; and if a pupil allowed his eyes to stray from the printed page, he was brought back to self-consciousness by the familiar reprimand, 'Look at your music'.

That playing from memory used to be confused with playing by ear (with possible 'faking') is suggested by the following passage from the delightful treatise *An Introduction to the Skill of Musick* (first published in 1654). 'To learn to Play by *Rote* or *Ear*, without Book', says the author, John Playford, 'is the way never to Play more than what may be gain'd by hearing another Play, which may soon be forgot; but on the contrary, he which Learns and Practises by Book, according to the *Gamut*, (which is the *True Rule* for *Musick*,) fails not, after he comes to be Perfect in those *Rules*, which guide him to play more than ever he was Taught or Heard, and also to play his Part in Consort, which the other can never be capable of.'

Even the experienced musician was considered unsafe without his notes; and as late as the year 1861, when Sir Charles Hallé was giving Beethoven recitals from memory, the critic of *The Times* accused him, not only of self-display, but of 'tempting the gods'. Although the new fashion of playing without notes was not welcomed by some players of the older school, including Clara Schumann (who, Amy Fay writes in 1873, 'cried over the necessity of doing it'), even the antagonism of critics had no effect. Grove's *Dictionary* tells us that Rubinstein (about 1886) 'went through the feat, for which he travelled without a note of music, of seven historical concerts'; that the 'prodigious musical memory' of von Bülow (trained by Liszt) 'enabled him also as a conductor to perform feats which had never before been attempted'. He was rivalled, however, by Richter, whose concerts in London (1879–81) 'excited much attention, chiefly for the conductor's knowledge of the symphonies and other large works, which he conducted without book'. But as Richter could do no wrong, there was no more to be said; and critics relaxed at last, surprised to find that, even without seeing music, they might yet listen to it in comfort.

Suggestion, doubtless, has played a part in the development of memory for music; custom has done the rest. Young people will usually do what is expected of them more readily if they see older people doing the same thing; and advanced students of to-day play even concertos from memory—a type of performance that to experienced artists of last century seemed either a prodigious feat or a complete impossibility.

Is there any advantage in playing from memory? Does it, as some believe, limit a performer's repertoire, as well as cause him unnecessary mental strain and anxiety? May it not be a fashion that will pass, like the crinoline, which, temporarily considered a necessity, has been wisely discarded? These are questions best answered by the performer himself; and although few are capable of analysing artistic experience, one of the greatest has done so. 'I have become convinced,' writes Busoni, 'as an old hand at this kind of thing, that playing from memory gives an incomparably greater freedom of expression. The player who is dependent on his notes, finds this not only limiting, but actually an interference. In any case, one must know the piece by heart if one is to give it the right shape in performance.'[1]

Busoni has stressed some of the advantages of playing without notes, but not all; and public opinion provides further good reasons for the continued popularity of the fashion.

It must be realized that any strain on the part of a performer will

---

[1] *Von der Einheit der Musik*, p. 81.

inevitably communicate itself to an audience; therefore, if the soloist is 'interfered with' by the written notes, the listener is robbed of his fullest enjoyment of music. Although, with the vast repertory now available, it is impossible for all musicians to find time to commit to memory every work played, yet there is no doubt that the public prefers a soloist to play by heart. Only very musical people shut their eyes when listening, and the public is affected (even unconsciously) by the look of the thing. Who has not been distracted from music by the anxious expression of some one 'turning over'? By merely glancing at a little book of words, a singer may lose touch with his audience, and when words or music are out of sight, both audience and performer are free to listen more attentively. In America, where the public not only prefers performance from memory but demands it, soloists (including many organists) consider memory a necessary part of their technique; and all should bear in mind that television is coming, and to stay.

But to perform from memory at home is one thing; to do so in public is quite another: the player may be able to execute a piece perfectly alone or before friends, but frequently in the public eye 'something goes wrong'; discouraged, he deplores his 'bad memory'.

If printed music is actually an interference, why should so many, including experienced artists, be afraid of appearing on the platform without it? If the player, to interpret a work to the best of his ability, must possess his music, in the sense of knowing it thoroughly, why should he dread memory failure? Let Busoni answer. 'Stage-fright affects the reliability of memory. When it comes, your head gets confused, and your memory insecure.' Busoni speaks from experience, and he speaks truly: fear of forgetting is due to nervousness, which may interfere with memory, bringing possible disaster even to the well-prepared. But does the presence of the score necessarily prevent nervousness? According to Busoni 'No'. 'If you have the notes to help you, then this stage-fright will take another form. Your touch gets uncertain; your rhythm is upset, and your tempo becomes hurried.' Even if printed notes prevent a break-down, it is evident that they cannot prevent the worst fault of all—unmusical playing, which, rather than performance from memory, may be described as 'playing without the music'.

What is the soloist to do? Is he to be interfered with by the written music, or is he to go on the platform without it, feeling as if his last hour had come? The possibility of a third course has not been considered except by a few artists who have found out for themselves a recipe for confidence. Although stage-fright with all its misery is usually taken for granted as a necessary price to pay for the privilege of self-expression, there are a few soloists who enjoy public appearance, in the sense of being stimulated by it; who, when warmed by excitement, find faith in memory amply justified. Like good actors who possess their part, they find memory, when trusted, an unfailing prompter.

This, then, is the alternative to being hampered 'with book' or nervous without—to engrave every detail of music on the tablets of memory, and to develop in memory a faith so complete that even adverse suggestions of the weaker-minded are powerless to shake it. Surely we can learn something from the musician with the prodigious memory, von Bülow, of whose work it was said: 'All details were thought out and mastered to the minutest particle; all effects analysed and calculated with the utmost subtlety, and yet the whole left an impression of warm spontaneity.' The psychological problems he solved are ours—they might well be termed 'doing' and 'being'. The study of psychology is yet in its childhood, and the practical application of it but newly born, but in time to come what may it not do for every worker?

A professional psychologist, Professor Aveling tells us, was employed to investigate the conditions of a factory. When his suggestions were acted upon 'The results were startling. Instead of an average of eighteen finished machines a day each, the output per worker rose to sixty-six machines. In other words, an increase of 266 per cent. was secured. The employees earned more wages; and there was no increase of fatigue.'[1]

The saving of time, the prevention of fatigue, how important are these to musicians, yet how rarely considered by teachers of music. Much practice is a 'trial' and its results an 'error'. Let us hope that teachers of the future will give as much attention to how pupils learn as is given now to what they learn. If, as has been proved by experiment, both time

[1] *Directing Mental Energy*, p. 33.

and energy may be saved by a learner of nonsense syllables, surely something can be done to help a learner of a Beethoven sonata.

If psychology can help the student, it can help the performer even more. There is wisdom in the proverb 'Nous sommes toujours à l'école'; and the true finishing school is a lonely school, where within narrow walls each one must learn a lifelong lesson of self-control. Instead of looking for support from without, the artist must learn to seek it within; and when he knows a work, in every sense, by heart, he will be able to turn attention inwards, and read the music there.

This book is an attempt to help the individual to find out for himself his best way of learning. Out of successful learning will grow faith in memory—a faith that will enable the performer to play his part, even 'in Consort'. Instead of dreading public appearance, he will learn to welcome it, as the great privilege it is, because, as Busoni says: 'For all whose calling it is to perform in public, memory is as little a hindrance as is the public itself.'

CHAPTER II

THE QUALITY OF MEMORY

MEMORY varies greatly in the individual both in quality and degree. One musician may be able to recall a piece more or less completely after hearing or playing it for the first time; another may take weeks to memorize the same piece. But the memory of the quick learner is not necessarily as accurate and retentive as that of the 'plodder', who, by absorbing music gradually, makes it truly a part of himself; while, in the process, he has time to make interesting discoveries concerning the music and its interpretation. Therefore, the slow learner may be safer in the long run.

'Natural' memory is usually associated with what is known as 'absolute pitch', though one with this gift is frequently in too much of a hurry to make the best use of it. Being able so easily to recall music heard or played, he is not always willing to undertake the conscientious study necessary if a piece is to be recalled at a future time, exactly as the composer wrote it.

It is evident that the memory of young people is highly impression-able; and even small children can repeat by heart whole pages of a book of which they may have grasped the sense but dimly. And because 'parrot' memory tends to disappear with the growth of self-conscious-ness, a theory has arisen that all memory deteriorates after the age of twenty-five, the age of maturity, many people (including not a few musicians) firmly convincing themselves that after thirty-five (at the very latest forty) it is useless to try to learn anything new. This belief in the decay of memory is highly convenient to the average mind, which is doubtless the author of it. Taking the line of least resistance, most people prefer to relax with the thought 'I am getting too old to learn' than to carry out the good resolution 'Every day I am going to learn something new'. Even if a person prides himself on his physique, he usually forgets (or does not wish to remember) that in order to retain youth, mind, like muscles, must have daily exercise.

There are, however, rare and lonely spirits preferring to take the line of most resistance; who, in spite of adverse suggestions of the mentally untrained by whom they are surrounded, refuse to allow an increasing number of birthdays to interfere with mental development. They realize that when the extreme facility of youth is left behind, its place may be filled by a power far more useful and reliable—the selective memory of maturity. In contrast to the musician of thirty-five who congratulates himself with the thought 'I am too old to concentrate' is to be found another type, joyfully undertaking a new sonata at the age of seventy or more.

Power of memory appears to depend upon the habit of learning more than is commonly supposed; and in memory's growing obedience may be found compensation for the passing of years. Like de Pachmann at seventy, who confessed he was only beginning to learn how to practise, the older musician may find a sense of adventure by tracing for himself new methods, new ways, new habits; retaining a youthfulness of outlook that will affect both memory and its counterpart, technique.

This book is not written for the lazy. If the musician does not naturally possess 'absolute pitch', he may have to work hard in order to remember music; another may have to work very little; but all must work. This, however, need not mean to 'slave', and the author is convinced that practice may be rendered more pleasant and more profitable than in the past. Concentration may be induced by interest, time saved by intelligent planning, and nervous strain avoided by rudimentary knowledge of mental law.

CHAPTER III

THE MEMORY QUARTET

MEMORY for music is not, as many think, a special kind of memory: it is a collaboration of memories possessed by every normal person—those of ear, eye, touch, and movement—and the well-trained performer of music usually makes use of them all.

1. *Aural Memory*

It seems hardly necessary to suggest that, of these, aural memory is the most important; but at one time music was presented to the beginner through the eye, instead of through the ear—as something to be seen, rather than heard. Even to-day some teachers encourage wrong habits in their pupils by making them look before they listen; consequently, those whose muscular memory is directed more by sight than hearing complain of having 'no ear'.

The four memories are to a great extent interdependent; they are also much affected by suggestion; consequently, if a player believes that his fingers cannot trust the guidance of his ear, he is conscious of a sense of inferiority, which will hinder progress in everything. Though it is possible to play some instruments without listening at all, if aural memory does not take precedence of muscular memory, performance is bound to be unmusical and uncertain. It is not always realized that aural memory may be developed in maturity; that any one whose ear-training has been neglected can improve habits of playing, even in later life, through the use of sol-fa, followed by study of harmony at the keyboard. Merely a few minutes of daily aural training will gradually lead the mind to think of music in terms of sound rather than in symbols of black and white. Then muscles will act less 'mechanically', and respond more readily to the thought of the player in relation to the sound he wishes to produce.

2. *Visual Memory*

The faculty for visualizing varies greatly in individuals. One musician may see a page of music in his mind's eye, very clearly, with no detail lacking; another may see the same page dimly, with many details missing; while yet another may not mentally see music at all; nevertheless, these last may be able to remember music every bit as well as the first, the keen visualizer.

For good sight-reading, visual memory is essential, but because a quick reader has no time to think consciously about the music, he is usually unable to recall it; which proves that music photographed in the mind's eye is not necessarily retained for long. Moreover, as those blind from birth can both learn and recall music perfectly without being able to visualize it, so can those who possess sight, and who do not see the music (or see it but vaguely) in their mind. Many teachers insist on their pupils' learning music by the look of it; but surely this is a mistake. If a pupil can 'hear with the eye', all is well; but another differently gifted may be seriously hampered by such training; and many have so worried their minds by endeavouring to memorize music in a way unnatural to them, that, believing they have a 'bad memory', they have given up memory-playing altogether.

The individual must decide for himself whether visual memory is necessary for him or not. One who naturally sees music in his mind's eye will be wise to use and to trust this form of memory; but another who prefers to rely on a keen aural and muscular sense can remember music equally well. Visual memory, like absolute pitch, can be very useful; but for the performance of music 'without book' it is not indispensable.

3. Tactual Memory

The memory of touch is best developed by practice with closed eyes, or in the dark. This will teach the player to listen more acutely, and also to feel his way; because, like the player of a clavichord, the pianist should learn to take hold of the keys neatly, instead of striking them. A good organist does not stamp on the pedals; he uses the groups of shorter pedals as a guide, and thus learns to feel his way without looking.

4. Muscular Memory

In the performer, muscular (or motor) memory must be highly developed, for without immediate nervous response to touch as well as ear, technical proficiency is impossible: although necessary movements should never become 'mechanical', they must become automatic, in the sense of subconscious. Only by learning to perform without looking can one fully realize how infallible can be this memory for movement, which includes a sense of direction. The physical ear hears the sound played; the inward ear determines what is to follow, and in response, the hands find their own way (if memory is trusted) through force of habit.

5. *The Mental Orchestra*

Memory of movement is virtually inseparable from that of touch; and to learn music at least three memories must collaborate—Aural, Tactual, and Muscular. Usually associated with these is Visual memory, which, either in the background or the foreground, completes the memory quartet.

These memories are leaders of the habits (without which no performance is possible)—a huge orchestra this, and a wayward, the members of which are for ever playing pranks, and delight in secret and subtle associations. It is for Intelligence, like a conductor, to train them, and their training demands not only understanding but discipline. Muscular memory, impatient of authority, is continually upsetting even the good habits. One bad habit, such as mind-wandering, can mislead the whole orchestra; and as all habits deeply resent interference, patient must the conductor be to make good use of the rehearsal hour. But habits are prodigiously responsive; if memories are interested, they will soon know their parts. If perfectly trained, they will perform perfectly, provided that Intelligence does not ever surrender place to the well-known deputy, Nervousness.

CHAPTER IV

THE OPEN MIND

THERE is no need for psychology to be the monopoly of the specialist; each one of us possesses a mind—a unique edition of the most practical psychology book available. It is true that many pages of our mental book are written in a language that as yet no one can interpret; but by reading between the lines we may learn, if little about the nature of mind, much about its manner of working. And as physical sensation proves a better teacher for the singer than the study of physiology, so will personal experience give more help to every student of music than knowledge theoretical.

We open our book of experience at Chapter I, on 'Dreams'—a chapter so crowded and complicated that it will require a lifetime of study; yet on the first page alone, we may glean much concerning memory.

Dreams may be sublime or they may be ridiculous; but, judged by standards of conscious thought, they are rarely reasonable; and when we fall asleep, we apparently hand over control of thought to another part of the self, which, for want of a better name, we call the subconscious. Thus we learn that our mind works on different planes, in different ways, according to the temporary scene of action. On waking, how can the musician dare to say 'I have no memory'? In his dream did he not meet some one consciously long forgotten—some one who sprang to life, recognizable in every feature, speaking with the voice of the living? Even a superficial study of dreams will prove that memory is extraordinarily retentive. Some psychologists go as far as to say that it retains every impression received.

The subconscious mind is also creative in character. The dream visitor we recognized so clearly is induced to do things that in life we never saw him do, to say things we never heard him say, by this mind in the background, which delights in taking any odd scraps of ideas and of combining them into fresh and fantastic forms. Consciously we cannot guess what it will think of next, or how it will react. On one occasion it may rejoice in a 'witticism', which, to the conscious mind, bears no semblance of wit; on another, it may provide a brilliant inspiration beyond the scope of consciousness. It may be overcome by a situation to the waking self merely laughable; or, forgetting human limitations altogether, including the law of gravity, it may enable the dreamer to float away from earth, as a matter of course. In dreams, our sense of values is changed, including our sense of time; and into half a minute may be compressed the experience of a month.

We shall find in our dream book many characters which may take control of subconscious action—not only angel, demon, and buffoon, but magician as well, who, in the right mood, is capable of solving almost any problem.

Subconscious activity can never cease; by night, as well as by day, to an accompaniment of endless dreams, the heart must beat, the lungs must breathe, tissues must be repaired. We take so much for granted— health, movement, capacity for speech; and because familiarity tends to rob us of wonder, let us, as conscious workers, sometimes pause to consider the miracle of living memory that controls the human body. As memory is our birthright, surely, rather than fearing its failure, may we not count on the perfection of its working? The act of speech, alone, is more complicated physiologically than that of playing a musical instrument; and if a musician can repeat one phrase of words from memory, to recall a phrase of music should be comparatively simple.

Musical performance, like speech, is 'acquired', which means that the necessary actions are not performed naturally (like the heart beat) but have to be learnt consciously. With effort we learn to talk, or write, or play a scale; but with practice such actions become easier; finally, so easy that we can perform them 'without thinking'. The performance from memory of a concerto appears to the uninitiated listener as nothing short of miraculous; to an experienced soloist it seems perfectly natural. The actual movements have lost nothing of their original complexity, but they become easy when direction is taken over by the 'habit mind', the subconscious.

Although conscious attention can be given only to one thing at a time, the subconscious mind is capable of directing simultaneously innumerable operations; and without its intervention our acquired actions would be wofully limited both in scope and character.

All learning resolves itself into the forming of habits, right and wrong; but at the outset the conscious mind is director of operations. It is for Intelligence to select material, to train habits, to criticize work done—a grave responsibility for the student who realizes the impressionability of mind and its native retention.

Although for practical purposes we may consider the mind as dual in character, we must realize that it is infinitely complex. Humbly the musician should study its working; and before the deep mystery of memory, he should try to keep, and in every sense, an 'open mind'.

CHAPTER V

TWO MINDS CO-OPERATE

MUSICAL achievement is impossible without the use of 'will power', but the most potent willing is a mental urge rather than a prodigious effort. There are, certainly, degrees of trying, involving more or less effort; but success in matters psychological is not necessarily brought about by fierce determination. We find, for example, if we try too hard to go to sleep, we remain awake; if we try not to be nervous, we become all the more so.

A valuable discovery was made by Coué, termed the 'law of reversed effort'. In the words of Baudouin: 'Whenever anyone is in the state of mind "I should like to, but I cannot", he may wish as much as he pleases; but the harder he tries, the less he is able.'[1]

1. *Conscious Interference*

Even if a counter-suggestion is not active, as in the case of 'reversed effort', conscious thought can seriously hamper subconscious action; if we try to play correctly when playing from memory, we merely succeed in making more mistakes than usual. The necessity for non-interference by the conscious mind is demonstrated in the case of all actions that have become habitual through repetition.

A man ties his tie so often that he can do it perfectly without thinking; but if he makes the mistake of giving attention to how he is doing it, he will tie a clumsy knot, and have to begin all over again.

Appearing on a platform, a speaker wishes to look unusually dignified; but conscious of his manner of walking, he walks stiffly, because unnaturally.

A trained typist, too intent on avoiding errors, will make an unusual number. It is surely unnecessary to give more examples of what may be termed 'conscious interference', because in our book of experience we can find so many; and if, when performing a piece, a musician thinks of his technique, instead of giving attention to what he is playing, he

---

[1] *Suggestion and Autosuggestion*, p. 86.

will invariably play badly, even with the music before him. Without music, conscious thought may cause a complete break-down of the machinery of memory.

Conscious interference, such as this, is not necessarily caused by fear (as in the case of reversed effort): it may be caused by ignorance concerning the sources of action. It has never occurred to some people that because life is very largely made up of habits mental and physical, there must be a part of the mind to take charge of these habits. Completely ignorant of subconscious possibilities, even experienced musicians sometimes confess they believe that responsibility for behaviour rests entirely with consciousness. The old idea of willing persists, along with the doctrine of perpetual effort.

2. *Passive Attention*

It cannot be repeated too often that the role of the musician's intelligence lies in selecting and educating the habits, in correcting them if need be; but there comes a stage when they must be allowed to work unimpeded. In other words, it is possible to carry thought too far. Conscious striving inevitably brings tension; and only when free from strain can the mechanism of memory (or recall) work unfailingly. Attention may then be termed 'passive'.

Consciousness, of which man is rightly proud, is but a small area of his mind. Behind it is the vastly older and more comprehensive mind, the subconscious, which can be trusted to play its part.

3. *A Marriage of Minds*

An experienced typist or knitter can use fingers so subconsciously that attention can be free to entertain itself with completely irrelevant thoughts; and because some kinds of typing and knitting require no attention, to occupy the conscious mind with something more varied may actually aid the work in hand—by allowing subconscious habits to proceed without interruption. But to play a musical instrument is a very different thing from using a machine; and though movements for playing should become automatic, in the sense that it is unnecessary to think of them, they should not become entirely 'mechanical'. The conscious mind should avoid interfering with subconscious working, it is true; but in performance that is musical the two minds cannot be divorced—in a subtle way they must co-operate.

4. *The Part of Attention*

Here we must ask ourselves an important question: 'In what consists the difference between automatic (free) playing that sounds musical, and playing (like the uncontrolled pianola) that sounds mechanical?' Because neither physiologist nor psychologist can yet solve this problem, let us consult our book of experience, where we find, not the answer to our question, but the reason for the difference between the two kinds of performance.

Any pianist gifted with technical facility is capable of playing a piece from memory, while, like a skilled knitter, reading an unfamiliar book —an experiment interesting as proof of the possible perfection and independence of muscular memory. But the resultant playing cannot be said to be musical in the sense of meaning a great deal; and because in this dual performance a player's mind must be given to the sense of what he is reading, no attention can be available for music. It is easy to surmise, therefore, that lack of meaning in the playing must be due to lack of attention. If, instead of music, we consider speech, we find the same rule holds good—when attention is absent, meaning is lost.

The writer had the painful experience of hearing a lecturer so afraid of forgetting his speech (learnt word for word) that he delivered it as fast as possible, in the monotonous voice of a ghost. His attention was obviously given, not to the sense of the words, but to the desirability of getting through an unpleasant task without disaster; as can be guessed, this lecture lacked significance, except as a lesson on how not to speak. But as words are the direct expression of meaning, few public speakers will be tempted to use them senselessly excepting the unintelligent guide, who, having repeated his monologue in parrot fashion for years, has lost all interest in it.

5. *Musical Meaning*

The meaning of music, however, is less limited than that of speech, and fully comprehended by comparatively few. Many, indeed, are carried away by performances that initiated musicians consider completely unmusical. The general public delights, above all, in speed; like a child, it can be hypnotized by showers of notes, musical in no sense but that they vary in pitch. You will hear people say 'I like music because it makes me think of so many things'; and though music can and does encourage mind-wandering in those who hear, but do not listen, for the truly musical it has a definite meaning, which, like the meaning of words, arrests attention. It is one thing to feel music; another to understand it; and yet another to speak its language with authority. There are temperamental players who exert too little conscious control (who rely entirely on emotion); there are cerebral players who think so consciously that they inhibit feeling; but the greatest artists exemplify a balance of feeling and intellect, when the two collaborate. This mental poise is something that cannot be taught, because it is the outcome of character.

6. *The Part of Character*

Habits of every day mould the musician's character, which, to a great extent, will decide his manner of playing and the behaviour of his memory. One who allows emotions to get out of control may lose control of technique; another who thinks too hard may interrupt memory; one obsessed by daily fears will be nervous at any time; while the scatter-brained at home is unlikely to achieve concentration on the platform. Only the musician with the balanced mind can be 'safe'. Practising concentration at all times, he will have no thought of self. Like a conductor, he will figuratively turn his back on his audience, and give himself up to the music of which he is medium: having trained and rehearsed his memories and habits by intelligent practice, he knows that he can rely on them to follow his musical direction.

CHAPTER VI

MENTAL VISION

WE open our mental book at the long chapter of 'Childhood', where among memories of study we find the teacher's familiar words 'Think what you're doing'. Thus early we learnt that attention has something to do with the mysterious process of learning, though how difficult it seemed to keep thoughts chained to a tiresome lesson, when outside was the attractive playground.

The teacher of music, however, was not insistent enough on the necessity for attention; turning to early memories of practice, we find records of the worst way of learning music—by muscular memory unaided by intelligence.

Adults, like children, can suffer from mind-wandering during practice, but many confess they feel powerless to canalize their thoughts. Taking the line of least resistance, they continue to learn music, as a child can learn what he does not understand, by dint of repetition. Unintelligent practice leads to performance uncontrolled; then the feelings upset the habits, which, in any case, are often uncertain of their parts; and memory is blamed for a break-down for which it is not primarily responsible.

1. *Mental Focus*

Concentration may be likened to mental vision, which can be focused by attention. Physically we see most clearly what we directly look at, though at the same time we see other objects less clearly. Likewise we think most clearly of an idea when we turn attention upon it, though frequently aware of other ideas on the fringe of consciousness.

The mind, like the eye, quickly tires if focused long on one point; restless by nature, it is ever preferably shifting attention. This mental need of change is supplied by the cinema, which can hold the attention of even uneducated people for hours on end. Music, too, gives infinite variety, and its moving sequence can occupy a music-lover's thoughts for a long period of time.

That some people possess more power of concentration than others is well known; also that it may be developed by exercise; but it is not always realized that concentration, as an attribute of memory, is the possession of every normal mind. By considering its most natural manifestations, we shall understand what brings it about.

2. *Spontaneous Attention*

Complete concentration is typified by a child when playing a game he loves; so absorbed is he that, for the time being, nothing else exists for him. That animals also experience concentration we can guess merely by watching a sporting dog on the scent of a rabbit. Obviously, 'spontaneous' attention arises when the object (or idea) upon which the mind is centred is associated with interest and enjoyment.

Older people, like children, concentrate naturally for periods of time varying with the attraction of the thing attended to. Not only the lover, but artist, scientist, and business man, may experience moments (possibly years) when emotion so intensifies interest that a person, idea, or ambition may become an obsession, occupying the mental field exclusively.

To practise with complete attention should not prove impossible, because music holds for the music-lover the chief motives for concentration—movement, interest, enjoyment, emotion, amounting to passion.

3. *Education*

How may we learn to bring about at will attention spontaneous and natural? Here again we may learn something from both children and animals—by considering their methods of training. Though a child can be made to attend temporarily to something that does not interest him, by a command, or by a threat of punishment for inattention, the modern teacher knows that this kind of education proves fruitless. It has been discarded also by the trainer of animals, even the lion-tamer having come to realize that his pupils learn least well under influence of fear. Affection can be made to replace antipathy, and the learning of the animal's task can be hastened by the incentive of a probable reward.

As fully conscious beings, we must understand that in self-education it is useless to fight with the child in us. Accepting the natural mind, we should patiently study it, as we would a pupil, humour, and reward it; only then shall we be able to direct it rightly.

The musician who finds concentration on work impossible should investigate his methods of practice. If necessary, he should courageously discard them all, and intelligently prescribe for himself a method more in keeping with mental needs.

4. *Degrees of Attention*

Interest is like a magnet (doubly strong if charged with emotion), which will always attract (or distract) attention. The will can forcibly drag it away, and centre it elsewhere; but as soon as control is relaxed, thoughts fly back to the point of interest, or to something, like a worry, which the mind prefers to think about through force of habit.

Ruling out the strained and tiring concentration described, there are two degrees of attention needful for practitioner and performer respectively. Let the musician first consider a picture that appeals to him. He can regard it in two ways—either by absorbing the picture, or by allowing it to absorb him. In the first case, he will analyse the work, consciously noting proportions, rhythm, lines, colour scheme, finally examining details in relation to the whole: in other words, he uses attention actively by thinking about the picture. In the second case, he will relax, take it in less consciously, by thinking of the picture. Consciousness no longer predominates; there is a steadying of attention, which leads to a balance of the two minds, a mental state by Baudouin termed 'contention'—'a psychological equivalent of attention, minus effort'.[1]

When regarding a picture passively, it is possible to allow one's sentiments to be affected more by subject than quality; when hearing music, one can dwell on day-dreams created by the sound; but because in both instances thought is led astray by personal associations, concentration on either picture or music cannot be complete.

Merely to gaze at a picture with interest will leave a mental impression, as will passive listening to music; but the power to recall either exactly demands keen observation and scrutiny. Even Mozart found his first impression of Allegri's *Miserere* to be incomplete; on second

[1] *Suggestion and Autosuggestion*, p. 142.

hearing, he had to make in his first edition both corrections and additions.

5. *Attention and Fatigue*

People differ in the length of time for which they can concentrate; and the power fluctuates in the individual, being greatly dependent on physical vitality. One who is tired, or who has just recovered from illness, must be patient; rather than work against his will, he should amuse himself by sight-reading, or by playing pieces he knows well: attention that is passive is less fatiguing than the active form.

The wise student will no longer try to fix attention. He will cease to worry about mind-wandering. Instead, he will add variety to·practice, and studying with intelligence he will find in music sufficient occupation for his thoughts. Provided he learns to cease work before he is tired, the usual kind of mind-wandering will no longer trouble him.

6. *Unwilling Attention*

Sometimes, however, the subconscious mind takes up the attitude of an obstinate child who says 'I won't learn this'. How is one to deal with such a mood? Like a child, the subconscious mind is sometimes surprisingly reasonable; if provided with an incentive, it can start the machinery of learning at full speed. Even in memorizing nonsense syllables (lacking both interest and association) it has been proved that an incentive in the form of a test can halve the necessary time for learning them.[1] In musical work an incentive is equally effectual. Attention can be arrested by the question 'How quickly can I learn this?' To take notes of time required adds the zest of a competition—with oneself. In the case of a difficult or uninteresting passage, it is a good plan to study it for only five or ten minutes a day; boredom is unlikely if the period is short and limited. In all work in which the urge to achieve seems lacking, an appeal should be made to self-interest, the magnet that never fails to attract attention. One should reason with oneself in this manner: 'By doing this thing well, I shall improve my power of concentration. By doing it as quickly as I can, I shall find more time for things I wish to do.' Simple arguments like these work wonders, and should always

[1] *Psychology and the Day's Work*, p. 255.

introduce the undertaking of those tasks in themselves distasteful, which have to be performed, nevertheless, by each one of us. The advice of William James is this: 'Be systematically heroic in little unnecessary points; do every day or two something for no other reason than its difficulty.'[1] Alas, the life of the artist provides sterner discipline than this. Yet the best of it is that a task apparently tiresome, if entered upon with zest backed by a definite reason for achievement, may prove to be surprisingly interesting.

7. *The Breath Pause*

Many students have learnt the necessity for keen attention, but fewer have learnt that when blunted by fatigue it will spoil the mental record. Though impossible to think about a piece too much, it is possible to think about one piece for too long. Centuries ago the Chinese realized the effect of familiarity; and even now they put an art treasure out of sight from time to time lest it lose significance for the beholder. The most ardent minds experience fatigue through lack of change; even the saints complained of what was called 'accidie', a mental state now commonly known by the less beautiful name of 'staleness'.

It is humanly impossible to focus attention all day; the keenest mind wanders for not a small portion of waking hours: like musical phrasing, attention requires the 'Luft Pause'. But to dream need not be a waste of time; and he who works little, and who concentrates, may do more in the end than another whose thoughts are never allowed to wander to fresh fields, where may be found the reward of reverie—new ideas. In the subsoil of the mind these are ever cropping up, though best perceived in a quiet moment. Among them a form, so rare, so hidden, that only the dreamer can find it. The name is Inspiration.

[1] *Talks to Teachers*, p. 75.

CHAPTER VII

MUSICAL THINKING

Two of the best interpreters may give of the same piece a completely different reading, which proves that an artist does not limit himself to written 'expression marks'; and as the letter of music is totally inadequate to express its spirit, each student must learn to make of every piece studied an edition of his own. This chapter, therefore, is an attempt to answer the question closely concerned with memory, 'How may one bring about playing in every sense musical?'

1. *Student and Artist*

An inexperienced student plays as he is taught, because he has not learnt to think for himself, and it follows that performance is unconvincing. A mature artist, on the contrary, plays in a certain way, because feeling tells him that way is right—for him; and his inner conviction expresses itself in every note.

The problems of musical interpretation resemble those of speech, because the means of expression alike include tempo, inflexion, and tone quality, in infinite variety. The speaker, however, requires no expression marks: the sense of words tells him inwardly how to use them. A good actor does not first learn the words of his part, adding a touch of expression here and there, as an afterthought; yet this is how many students learn their notes, giving much more attention to a secondary factor such as fingering than to the essential, phrasing, which determines so much, including good fingering.

2. *Musical Thought*

All artists must create a thing mentally in order to give it outward form; and as the painter sees his work in his mind's eye before reproducing it, so should the musician create a mental conception of music he is about to play. As Matthay says: 'Listening does not mean merely hearing what the automatic centres manage to do . . . effective listening implies pre-listening all the time as to what should

23

be.'[1] The necessity for this is forced upon the singer, who, to sing in tune, must place a note mentally before producing it; but a pianist may be tempted to use his fingers as a typist usually does—through muscular and tactual memory alone. Agreed that the pianist should 'think' music as well as play it, how is he to learn to do this, especially if he has formed the habit of mind-wandering during practice? How is attention to be brought to bear on each note, without interfering with technique? In the expression of both words and notes, stress plays an important part; and by first considering it, the player will more easily solve his problem.

3. *Stress*

In music, as in books, one finds italics, where a writer asks for special emphasis by underlining individual notes, as in the phrase below. This should be sung (with crescendo), preferably using French time-names; then played (without counting); and when stressing individual notes, the player will realize that he is giving attention to their increasing tone, singing them inwardly this time instead of audibly.

To think a note, therefore, is to 'place' it; and more attention is necessarily given to sound than to technique (the manner of using finger and key). Thus there is a great difference between thinking notes and thinking *of* notes, in the sense of naming them. The former brings about playing musical and controlled; the latter, unmusical playing, with probable failure of memory through conscious interference. In the first case, it is true, a margin of attention will be available for touch; while creating sounds, the player will also be conscious of the sensations of playing. In one way a musical pianist resembles a typist who, when making a number of carbon copies, must use each key with a certain degree of attention in order to give sufficient stress; and a good player, also, controls touch according to the quality of sound (the musical letter) he wishes to produce.

[1] *Musical Interpretation*, p. 7.

4. *The Note of Conviction*

In music, as in speech, sounds receive a variety of stress; some are not stressed at all; but no note, however short, should be played perfunctorily; and in the phrases below, even a demisemiquaver (32nd note) has significance as forming a prefix to the accent following. The student should think these phrases silently, by hearing the sounds mentally; then play them, singing the sounds inwardly as before.

Ex. *a.* Brahms, Op. 90.

At sight, one player may be capable of foretelling pitch, but not time; another may foretell time, but not pitch; but in familiar music, every one ought to be able (like the best sight-reader) to predetermine pitch, time, and tone quality.

To prove that he is thinking music, the student should play very slowly a passage he knows well; and if he can hear each note (or chord) mentally before playing it, he is performing in the right way. The clarity arising through mental control is particularly telling 'on the air'; and every broadcaster should bear in mind that listeners at a distance cannot be deceived by speed. The unseen public asks, above all, for distinctness and meaning.

5. *Counting*

French time-names will greatly help the beginner in mentally placing notes, because with each is consciously associated a spoken syllable. 'One and two and one' was the old-fashioned attempt to make such an association; but this method provided no syllables for the smaller divisions of the beat; and time patterns, like those above, are rarely reproduced as accurately by a soloist as by an orchestral player: French time-names help to give each note its exact duration.

It must be clearly understood, however, that all forms of counting are merely preliminary guides to habit; if not discarded, they may defeat their own end. Pupils, for example, who persist in counting aloud when practising will feel lost without this mental support in the examination room. During practice, one should think a phrase, counting audibly, if necessary; then play without counting, allowing the sense of time to guide the movements inwardly.

6. *Musical Speech*

In very rapid performance, needless to say, thinking and doing become almost simultaneous: a player has to think sounds in groups, as a quick typist thinks letters. In written speech, letters are grouped into words; but unfortunately, the usual notation of music (which groups notes into blocks, according to the beat) leaves gaps on paper between beats, where the ear should hear no gap. Contrast the usual grouping of notes with that in the passages below, where notes are linked as they should be linked mentally—with no break before an accent.

Ex. *b.* Schumann, Op. 7.

Ex. *c.* Scriabin, Op. 31, No. 1.

In written speech, groups of words are made clear to the eye through punctuation, and curved lines called 'phrase marks' are supposed to make clear the groups of sounds in music. But much piano music is decorated with phrase marks that have no connexion with musical punctuation; and the matter is further complicated by the frequent misplacing of bar-lines. Theoretically, these are supposed to point out the coming strong accent, as they do in the phrases below, 'barred' according to musical notation.

To | *be,* or | *not* to be; | *that* is the | *question*:

But in music we are confronted with problems like this:

Ex. *d.*   Bach, Prelude, Bk. 1, No. 22.

Here we find misplaced bar-lines, which stress the wrong beats; also misplaced phrase marks, which make breathing-points where no singer would breathe. This is just as senseless as to write the words of Shakespeare thus:

| *To*; be or not, | *to* be; that, | *is* the; question:

It is not surprising that some students find difficulty in remembering their music, because they do not understand what they are trying to express. What, then, is the learner to do? How is he to edit music so that he may interpret it clearly for others?

Firstly, it should be realized that the small musical group (musical word) usually begins before the bar-line, and if written in speech would look like this:

To b | e, or no | t to be;

Compare this with Ex. *b* and *c*, p. 26, where the arrangement of notes suggests music's onward urge—its rhythm. Students are referred to Matthay's book *Musical Interpretation,* in which will be found explicit directions for bringing about rhythmical playing. Time (the arrangement of beats weak and strong) is not to be confused with rhythm, the continuous movement of which might well be likened to the sinuous movement of a snake.

7. *Phrasing*

Within this progression we find a series of curves, both big and small, the shaping of which is decided by phrasing. The end of one curve may be the beginning of another curve; or it may be a definite breathing-point. (See Examples *e* (below) and *a*, p. 25.)

Ex. *e*. Chopin, Op. 66.

Thus phrasing might be likened to the progression of the looper cater-pillar—a movement towards a definite point, from which another progression begins. These curves are always present, whether marked or not, and musical people unconsciously feel them. An unmusical player will think the beats of a waltz thus: *1* 2 3   *1* 2 3; a musical player will think them in this manner: $\overline{1\,2}$ $\overline{3\,1}$ 2.

8. *Memory and Phrasing*

It is possible to learn music intellectually, and so thoroughly that one may be able to write it all out with the aid of photographic memory. But to be able to perform music learnt is quite another matter. This involves habits; and if students form the stumbling habit, musical thinking hesitates. Yet, if in rapid passages attention is given less to the note as a unit, and more to its place in a musical group (syllable, word, or phrase), the worst technique will become more fluent.

It will now be understood how important is the right grouping of notes in the learning of them. To begin with, it is easy to learn something that looks short and that sounds tuneful; then, because memory and technique depend on chains of thought, it is understandable, if a musical link is missing, that both may come to grief. String players usually phrase more musically than pianists; perhaps because bowing suggests the onward movement of music; perhaps because the instrument's tone resembles the human voice. Physical breathing gives continuity to notes sung; and if the voice is used as guide, a student will instinctively know which sounds to stress, which to group together, and where to make the breath pause.

Below are given a few passages in which the smaller groups are suggested by dotted lines; but the end of a curve should not disturb the time; neither should it break the legato, as would the end of a phrase mark.

Ex. *f.* Beethoven, Op. 27, No. 2.

Ex. *g.* Bach, Prelude, Bk. 2, No. 2.

Ex. *h.* Chopin, Op. 28, No. 19.

Ex. *i.* Bach, Prelude, Bk. 2, No. 6.

Where there are alternatives, intelligence as well as the voice can be helpful. In Ex. *j*, although groups are rhythmical, the second arrangement is preferable, because passing-notes return to harmony-notes before the end of a group.

Ex. *j.* Chopin, Op. 66.

In all playing, it is essential, as Matthay says, to think towards an accent, instead of away from it, as many are led to do by the appearance of musical notation. Compare the examples below, where a rearrangement of notes helps to suggest the forward movement of music. (Groups of melody notes are indicated by dotted lines.)

Ex. *k*. Bach, Prelude, Bk. 2, No. 15.

Allegro vivace

N.B. Throughout this book, none of the dotted lines are to be blindly accepted: players differ in the way in which they feel phrasing. The essential is that, within longer lines, notes should be grouped in smaller curves, both mentally and rhythmically.

9. *Dual Attention*

There is no better guide to phrasing than the voice; but to sing incessantly while practising is a habit difficult to relinquish in public, and one distracting for any audience. Besides, while singing, the player will give himself up too much to feeling; his attention will be less detached, less critical, than if centred entirely on the music he is making. Audible singing should be used by an instrumentalist merely as a tone pattern for phrasing, and should usually precede the playing, rather than accompany it.

As suggested, musical attention is dual in character: we listen to what we are doing, and at the same time we think ahead, because mentally creating the sound before it happens. A good conductor, besides being an actor, is also a prophet. While directing the passing music, he creates for the orchestra, by means of his movements and by his eyes, the shape and mood of the phrase to come.

II

CHAPTER VIII

IMPRESSIONS IN THE MAKING

MANY students ask the question, 'When am I to begin memorizing?' To this there is only one answer: 'The next time that you practise.' Even when practising without thinking, we memorize, in the sense that we train the wrong habits.

A student whose memory is 'bad' should take a great deal of trouble to improve his method of learning, because upon the quality of practice depends to a great extent the behaviour of memory.

The study of a piece resolves itself into three processes:

1. Training the memories (registration of impressions).
2. Training the habits (association).
3. Practice of performance (recall).

1. *Mental Photography*

What do we remember? That which we notice. What do we notice? That which arrests our attention. The subconscious mind registers impressions without the aid of attention; but to be able to recall these at will, we must consciously supervise the making of mental pictures.

How clearly do we remember the first music lesson, the first examination, the first public concert: the clarity of these pictures in our book of experience will bring home to us the extreme importance of all first impressions. But many students read a new piece through 'just anyhow', to get an idea of 'how it goes', not realizing that if the first reading is incorrect, the piece may never go really well. A wise learner will rather take the advice of the Romans, and 'make haste slowly', because when first impressions are clear, accurate, and musical, much of the work is done. To subconscious memory nothing is unimportant. Every wrong note, every mis-reading, every break at an unmusical point is recorded, faintly, if attention is wandering, but recorded, nevertheless. This will make the student think, which is precisely what he ought to do; and he must continue to think very hard until necessary habits are trained.

31

At a first rehearsal a conductor will not hand over to his players the parts of a new score without having thought about it, because until then, he is not in a position to tell them what to do. Likewise, before playing a new piece as a whole, the student should try to find out something about it: form is the outline of a musical picture; mood will determine quality. Big lines should be blocked out, and smaller lines (the phrases) defined; after which, details can be added. In the case of a new work, every good conductor gives a great deal of time at a first rehearsal to phrasing. So should the performer, associating fingering with phrasing; because habits, like memories, cling tenaciously to first impressions. Does not every one know by experience how difficult it is to alter a fingering practised? Even if one superimposed is better, the previous habit may return as soon as conscious control is relaxed.

As self-teachers we should be very conscientious at our first rehearsals; we should keep sight-reading confined to special material for the purpose; we should postpone performance of a piece until habits are quite certain of their parts. And just because a new piece tends to rouse interest, let us make the most of the 'drive' that novelty gives to the learning of everything, including music.

CHAPTER IX

TRAINING THE HABITS

MANY musicians complain that they have no memory, because, after learning a passage, they find they cannot recall it the next day. If the first impression is vivid, there is less likelihood of forgetting; but to learn a piece of music is a very complicated matter, which necessarily takes time. If one were asked to draw a crowded map from memory, one would not expect to remember it perfectly at first glance: one would have to go over the first impressions, possibly many times, in order to deepen them; and each time more and more attention could be given to detail.

Every student should be patient when first learning a piece. No impression is lost; the second will 'take' more readily, the third still more readily: the mind learns with a crescendo of speed if repetition is rightly spaced. But repetition, though necessary, cannot take the place of conscious thought; and here many students make their chief mistake. In order to memorize a map, to look at it frequently will not be enough: to recall the shapes exactly, one must think about them, comparing one feature with another. The courses of two rivers, for example, are somewhat alike, but we notice differences; and the comparison will help us to remember our map. This, then, is the only way to remember music with certainty—to analyse it, making conscious associations. Here are two passages that begin the same but which end differently; here is a phrase ending on the dominant, in contrast to another that ends on the tonic. One recalls at will only what one notices, and nothing more.

1. *Rehearsal*

When memories have a clear impression of the music, habits must be trained; but which? There is a very large number to choose from, including the feelings, which, unrestrained, will overwhelm the orchestra. This was the experience of Paderewski, who writes: 'It took me half my life to realize that there are two ways of using the piano. The one way is to play, the other is to work. If you use the one, you will never achieve

anything. . . . You can be drunk in any art on your own emotion. **And,**
alas, a great many people are wasting their time that way; arriving at **no**
result at all.'[1]

It is true that no player can dispense with feelings, but to make others
feel, one must give precedence to habits of expression, trained by means
of thought, and tempered by judgement.

Among students are to be found two types—one who considers that
to enjoy music is the same thing as to express it; another, so intent on
learning notes that he gives no thought to music. Some teachers make
their pupils practise a new piece 'without expression', but what is
the object of such training? An unmusical practitioner is unlikely to
perform musically, without changing his habits, which is not easy at
any time.

2. *Expression and Memory*

If a phrase is meant to be soft, why practise it loudly? To play softly
is not easy, because requiring strict control of kinaesthetic habits.

Why should a melody be practised as a succession of 'even' notes,
if the composer intends it to sing, with varied tone, above a soft accompaniment? For pianists, this means co-ordination of habits: one hand
may have to produce simultaneously different qualities of tone, involving
different types of touch; and it is useless to leave the practice of delicate
muscular adjustments until the week before a concert.

Again, if a passage consists of four notes to the beat, why should it
be rehearsed in triplets? In technical exercises, mental control can be
learnt through variation of accent; but in a piece, surely the essential is
to practise a passage with the rhythm designed by the composer. There
is even a method requiring that the right-hand part should be played by
the left hand, and vice versa; and though this type of practice may help
a student to notice things in music, it cannot help him in the second stage
of work, which consists of training habits in the way they should
perform.

Apart from other considerations, expression is a great help to
memory. Actors with the best memory for words are those who concentrate on their meaning, associating with it their expression through

[1] *My Story.*

voice and gesture; and as we all tend to remember what is associated with emotion, musicians should, at the first rehearsal of any piece, associate expression with every note played.

3. *Simplification*

When a student sets to work, he should remind himself that he is temporarily a teacher, and that his pupils (the habits) should be taught, like modern pupils, with consideration: this means that learning should be simplified as much as possible. Indeed, the secret of learning may be said to consist of the faculty of attending to one thing at a time. Students frequently try to learn a dozen things simultaneously, changing fingering and phrasing from day to day, so that the habits get utterly bewildered. Is it surprising that some people fail to remember what they practise? Below is the kind of passage that few learn correctly, because it requires a combination of difficult habits.

Ex. *a*. Beethoven, Op. 27, No. 2.

Here one should copy the conductor, who at first rehearses his orchestra in part only; and by training habits in small groups, it will be found much easier to co-ordinate them afterwards. The above passage becomes at once understandable if voices are divided between two hands. (The bass may be practised alone.) Attention will be temporarily free to decide phrasing, legato, staccato, tone colour.

Ex. *b*.

4. *Stress of the Bar*

Bars, like beats, are not equal in strength, and it is essential to feel the musical stress. In quick pieces, especially, an equal stress on every strong accent breaks up the rhythm, making music difficult both to remember and to play. In Ex. *a*, strong bars (defined by the harmony) are marked by a double line above the staff.

5. *Finger Legato*

A division of parts is always to be recommended at the beginning, because it gives the student an opportunity to hear what the music should sound like. He will then say, 'How am I to obtain the same result when two parts are played by one hand?' Now is the moment to arrange a fingering that will carry out the musical idea. (To divide voices in Ex. *b* cannot record a wrong fingering, because the left hand will eventually be required elsewhere.) A preliminary division of labour prevents the appearance of many bad habits, including that of over-pedalling. In the passage below, the beauty of sustained notes can be best appreciated by first separating the parts; and because pedal is undesirable here, fingering must be chosen to agree with the required legato.[1]

Ex. *c*.

Ex. *d*. Debussy, Prelude, Vol. 1, No. 8.

---

[1] The use of the damper pedal is fully explained in the author's *Musical Secrets*.

6. *Beauty of Detail*

Taking one thing at a time, the student will begin to see the significance of many things that hitherto had never caught his attention. How much meaning, for example, is added to the bass below by one semiquaver (16th note). To notice such things makes one remember them.

Ex. *e.* Beethoven, Op. 57.
Andante con moto

7. *Second Impressions*

Conscious control should not be relaxed too soon, and attention should go over the lines of our musical chart, deepening impressions, perfecting detail, supervising habits.

Although one should choose the easiest way of doing things, the musical way is not always easy. For instance, in Ex. *a*, p. 35, it is simpler to play either staccato or legato throughout; but the composer wishes otherwise, and attention cannot be free to conduct performance until the fingers can automatically do what music requires of them.

If one lingers over the first stages of learning, every piece will provide possibilities of improvement. One should continually ask oneself questions like these: 'Is the bass giving enough support? Is the climax coming too soon? Are there any beautiful details I have overlooked?' Critical attention is necessary at every hour of rehearsal.

The mood of music decides the manner of expression. For instance, if a piece is marked *tenebroso*, it is not enough for the performer to imagine 'darkness'; the audience must hear a dark tone, with bass predominating. Again, in the 'Moonlight' Sonata, to suggest a quiet mood to others, the musician's tone should be both subdued and even, under a melody that does not disturb the rhythm.

8. *Repetition*

Every time one takes out a piece, one can discover how to make improvements in the expression of it, including more subtle shades of tone quality. Indeed, a piece is never 'finished', because its possibilities enlarge with the player's mental outlook. This is one of the reasons why no piece should be practised for too many days on end: repetition, unless intelligently planned, may even prevent the improvement of habits.

There is no virtue in practising for eight hours a day. Conscious work is tiring; and though professional musicians have to put an extra strain upon themselves occasionally, no one should practise, as a rule, for more than three or four hours daily. Until a student has learnt how to practise well he should limit himself to one hour, dividing it into four short periods of concentrated work. It does not take long to repeat a passage two or three times, and with critical attention focused on a predetermined aspect of the music, thoughts cannot wander, and work will be well done. (See also Rules, p. 51.)

9. *Imaginative Practice*

A good serial story breaks off at an exciting moment in order to stimulate the reader's curiosity; and if a practitioner can cease rehearsal when interest is keen, he will return to work at the next opportunity with added zest. Of course, when in a good mood for study, it is often inadvisable to interrupt one's train of thought; but it is essential to cease practice before the approach of boredom.

Every musician should allow his conscious mind a holiday from practice, preferably once a week: an occasional rest or change of occupation is a physical and mental necessity. But subconscious activity never ceases. Muscles develop after exercise; and the mind, apparently resting, assimilates material provided during the practice hour; in the mental dark-room, associations are fixed in a mysterious way, and time must be allowed for this important part of mental development.

When words are read silently, movements take place in the small muscles of the throat; and when music is rehearsed silently, though movements are inhibited, there is no doubt that impressions are made on the nerve tracts. Does one not experience sensations in the finger-tips proving this?

A concert singer, out of necessity, does much work silently, and an instrumentalist, also, should frequently think a passage or piece, instead of playing it. Experienced singers rarely use their full voice in practice, and instrumentalists, too, should save themselves by keeping tone within certain limits. To practise quietly, to make every shade of tone within a forte, quickens the ear, besides preventing mental and physical fatigue.

No practice room should contain a noisy clock. One who really listens to music may find even the ticking of a watch an unbearable accompaniment.

10. *Mistakes*

A slip in practice should not be confused with a mis-reading, and in the later stages of practice an occasional slip matters less than the interruption of mental associations, which leads to stumbling. Here again, one should copy the conductor, who at later rehearsals will refrain from pulling up his orchestra needlessly. Mentally noting faults, he will continue until the end of a musical section; then, after discussing possible improvements with his players, he will repeat the whole passage. This is the best way to practise music that is becoming familiar—in musical sections, breaking up chains of thought as seldom as possible.

11. *Changing Habits*

If the same slip recurs, the situation is more serious, and it is useless to repeat a faulty passage again and again, hoping that it will come right eventually. Instead, one should try to find out the cause of every such mistake, because habits, like some orchestral players, are inclined to be lazy when the conductor's eye is not upon them; though rightly trained, they may prefer to take the line of least resistance. A reason should always be given for the correction. For example, if the fingering habits have altered the original instructions, it must be clearly understood that the first fingering is necessary to avoid a break in a particular group of notes. A conscious association, such as this, will encourage the best habits.

If, on examination, a slip proves to be a real mistake (a wrong record), one must rehearse the memories carefully—give them another, a clearer mental picture along with a reason for the alteration. If a false note has been recorded, the right note should be pointed out in relation to others, harmony providing valuable associations for the correction of first impressions. But this kind of fault is difficult to eradicate; after patient rehearsals, both memories and habits may revert quite unexpectedly to their original reading.

The mistake of trying to 'break' a habit may upset the whole orchestra; even to draw attention to a bad habit, such as stumbling, makes matters worse than before. Therefore, if a student has the habit of stiffening (one which will hamper every member of the orchestra), the less attention he gives it the better; he should concentrate, instead, on the inseparable habits of mental and muscular freedom. In altering any habit, the essential is to make a reason for the change; to concentrate wholly on the new habit; and to forbid subconscious performance until, through thoughtful practice, that habit is confirmed in good ways.

Watchful attention can prevent the appearance of many unnecessary habits. Paderewski tells us how he used to practise for hours before a looking-glass in order to achieve the impassive expression he so often missed in the faces of other artists. It is by studying the book of experience of other people, by watching their habits, that one may learn which to cultivate: one is not always the best judge of one's own.

12. *The Orchestral Habit*

Some of the finest instrumentalists have the advantage of being experienced conductors. Unfortunately, some pianists and singers rarely listen to an orchestra except 'on the air'; consequently, when they come to perform with the real thing, they do not feel at ease, and memory can be upset by the unexpected. If a singer is unprepared for the proximity of the strings, he may be put out by a part of the accompaniment that he has never noticed in the piano version. A concerto player, dependent on a cue easily recognizable on a second piano, may wait for it in vain on the platform, because, from where he is seated, it may not be audible. Every ambitious student, therefore, should cultivate the habit of attending, not only orchestral concerts, but rehearsals, where, provided with a score, he can become familiar with the sonority and placing of instruments, and much besides. This experience will provide a mental background that will give freedom to all good habits when the opportunity of concerted work materializes.

SELF-QUESTIONS FOR THE PRACTITIONER

1. Do I practise when I am tired? *Sometimes - Regularity important.*
2. Do I practise with my mind full of other things? *Seldom.*
3. Do I practise for too long at a stretch? *No*
4. Do I despise the short practice period? *Yes* *pretty - depends how short.*
5. Do I make any scheme of work? *Yes*
6. Do I attend to the expression as much as to the notes? *Try*
7. Do I try to find out shades of meaning not indicated by expression marks? *Sometimes differ from expression mks*
8. Do I divide music for practice into phrases or musical sections?
9. Do I stop in the middle of phrases? *Seldom*
10. Do I try to find out the cause of a mistake? *always*
11. Do I pause between repetitions? *mostly*
12. Do I count the repetitions I make? *No*
13. Do I find it as interesting to practise an old piece as a new one? *Yes*

CHAPTER X

PERFORMANCE FROM MEMORY

No rule can be laid down concerning the amount of time necessary for the first stages of work: the individual must decide for himself when sufficiently well prepared to perform subconsciously.

1. *Testing the habits*

Before a piece is mastered it is advisable to test the habits—to find out how far their training has advanced. Between analytical repetitions, passages (occasionally the whole piece) should be performed without interruption. The last stage, playing 'without book', should be postponed until habits are proficient.

A student usually clings to printed music because he does not really know it. He realizes, perhaps just before an examination, that he has learnt his pieces in the wrong way—by muscular memory unaided by intelligence. Naturally he is nervous; but if he does not interfere with his habits, he will probably 'get through somehow', more safely, indeed, than another who dare not let himself go.

2. *Freedom*

Even with music before them, many people never learn to play freely; mental strain shows itself in tenseness of facial expression, posture, and in tone quality as well. Some have a theory that what is difficult is good for one; others despise what can be done without effort; but the apparent ease of the best performer is hardly earned, and can be demonstrated only after years of painstaking study.

To relax muscles helps to relax the mind; but during performance, complete relaxation is, of course, impossible, because this would mean utter collapse of technique. (One who completely relaxes his mind, falls asleep.) 'Freedom' is a better word for the desired muscular condition, which helps to bring about the right mental state, 'attention minus effort': when mind and body are free from strain, their habits perform with most proficiency. If consciously thinking of neither notes nor technique, if hands and fingers find their way automatically, one is performing in the right way.

It is not always easy to relax the minds of those who have never played subconsciously. But nearly every one can play at least a scale from memory, and the sensation of playing without thinking can be used as a basis for further memory-playing. Sometimes it is enough merely to think a phrase in order to be able to reproduce it from memory: to distract attention from the notes is the chief matter. To relax the facial muscles is alone a help towards subconscious playing; and to try to play from memory with closed eyes (or in the dark) is the best test of all, because impossible if one is mentally tense.

3. *By Heart*

To learn music by thinking about it is comparatively easy; but to learn to perform without thinking is for many people more difficult. In the first stage one is absorbing the music; in the second, one should be absorbed by it. Mood, feeling, these are subconscious, and to express them the musician has to turn attention inwards. One conductor, who never doubts his memory, visualizes music, not on the pages of a score, but on a long scroll, which passes before his mental vision.

How is consciousness to be occupied? There is so much going on in music, and in a piece like a fugue it is impossible to follow every part with equal attention; nor is this necessary. A conductor looks at different players in turn; though hearing them all, he is giving his chief thought to an entry, or to a special musical effect. And the performer's attention also can turn to different aspects of music with great rapidity; at one instant he may be supremely conscious of the melody; at another, of the bass, of pedalling effects, perhaps; yet, round the focal point, music as a whole is within the field of consciousness; all is heard, though one part may be more keenly listened to than others.

Excitement brings with it hyperaesthesia; and sometimes the performer may experience an unusual lucidity of mind along with a strange sense of detachment. Consciousness seems to stand aloof, as if watching operations, and a thought may cross the mind—'Is it really I who am making this music?'

4. *Interrupting the Habits*

When sight-reading one is forced to think unconsciously of music that lies ahead of one's fingers; but consciously to do this when playing by heart is the greatest mistake of all. In the experience of nearly every public performer is to be found a painful memory caused by the question of consciousness, 'What note, what passage is coming next?' Interfered with by doubt, habits of course break down; and the shattered musician blames memory, when all that is wanting is faith.

It will now be understood why it is so important to consider the end of music (interpretation) before the means. Instead, if one concentrates on learning mere notes, the mind will cling to that first impression; and to think of actual notes, when playing by heart, nearly always causes a break-down of memory. Why, we cannot say, but it does. When a performer begins to doubt his memory, he should say to himself 'Relax'. Attention should be turned immediately to the rhythm, to the mood, to any aspect of music that will prevent conscious interference.

But if associations are broken, and the mental thread is lost, what is to be done? An unintelligent guide, interrupted in his harangue, has to begin all over again in order to 'find the place'; but it is extremely painful for every one at a concert if a soloist has to repeat the first portion of a piece (perhaps several times) in order to finish it. Surely, if musical form were clearly understood, this could never happen; in any case, an intelligent musician ought to be able to start his orchestra, not only at section A, but also at X, Y, or Z.

A lapse of memory is frequently caused by interference with habits during rehearsal. Although it is wise to separate musical parts when first learning them, to do so after habits are co-ordinated will necessarily upset subconscious arrangements; and the memory of those who have 'absolute pitch' is especially liable to be disturbed by the practice of separate parts after learning the whole.

It is also disturbing to memory to write out music learnt: to do this certainly proves that one knows the notes, but through making these too conscious, one may be unable to play them subconsciously. Rehearsing the notes (naming them mentally) is equally dangerous: to draw attention to notes is the last thing one ought to do; and on this account it is better not to practise just before a concert, because one may ruin passages that the subconscious mind knows perfectly well. It requires strength of mind to cease work at such a time, but the result justifies faith in memory.

5. *Reviving Impressions*

However familiar a piece, it should be rehearsed carefully from time to time with the printed copy. Revision strengthens the memory of natural visualizers, besides preventing subconscious alteration of music learnt. (A piece always played by heart tends to change slightly, like a folk-song.) Revising an old piece, one makes fresh discoveries on the familiar page; after months, perhaps, the key is found to a passage hitherto incomprehensible; and one exclaims with surprise, 'Why did I never notice this before?' Thus we learn that thoughtful work is not wasted; through having grown mentally we now see significance in things that previously had no meaning; and of all lessons the careful revision of an old piece is the most encouraging.

6. *Tempo and Memory*

It is sometimes advisable to 'think' a slow piece more quickly than written, because this helps to make the musical lines clearer. Though easier technically, slow music is more difficult to play from memory than quick, because the conscious mind has more time to interfere with subconscious operations; therefore, it is helpful to play it at first more quickly than written. On the contrary, quick music may be slowed down to give opportunity for study of detail. And as it is not easy to play a rapid piece from memory very slowly indeed, a final rehearsal adagio should be used as a test of one's capacity of performing quick music 'without book' and without thinking.

7. *First Performance*

If you have never played from memory (or only very little), do not at once undertake a complete sonata; much better practice is provided by little pieces or by variations, because these look short. Before too big a helping mental appetite disappears; and all tasks should be presented to the mind in tempting portions easily assimilated. When you can play a few easy pieces from memory, your mind will be prepared for something longer, but not until then.

If you can play a piece from memory fluently when alone, you know it; but do not be discouraged should you make mistakes when you first play it to others. Such faults are usually due, not to failure of memory, but to lack of practice in performing: many slips are caused by nothing but self-consciousness. Only by learning to give attention to music instead of to the possible criticism of an audience, can one learn to play safely by heart. The first stage of work is making things happen; the last is allowing things to happen; and there is a world of difference between the two.

INTERLUDE

'REHEARSAL'

Characters:

INTELLIGENCE (the Conductor)
THE MEMORIES
THE HABITS AND THE FEELINGS

In the Pianist's Studio

THE curtain rises on the mental orchestra. In the foreground are the memories. Behind them are countless habits, some old and skilled in music, others new and undisciplined.

The memories stand out, clear in outline, with expressions thoughtful, yet stern.

The habits are almost expressionless, which makes them appear more stupid than they are. The new habits are hardly distinguishable in outline (all are dressed in grey); but practice develops them, and the older they grow the more definite they appear. Among them is the Sense of Time, who used to be placed with the feelings. But, owing to his interference with Rubato, he was moved to a separate desk, where, black with time, he dominates the orchestra.

The feelings are indescribable, because they are always changing. The deepest feelings cannot be hidden. Through the oldest habit, their colours shine, shifting with the music like a moving rainbow.

PRÉLUDE No. 20

CHOPIN

From the Oxford Original Edition of Frédéric Chopin.

Apart from Time, who sits erect and rigid, the whole orchestra is very restless. Before it stands the conductor, Intelligence. He is examining the score with eyes both 'intro' and 'extravert'. In his hand is his baton, Attention. He raises it, and there is the silence of expectancy. Then he speaks:

Good morning, gentlemen. To-day we rehearse a new piece (*a murmur of disapproval among the habits*)—the 20th Prelude of Chopin. (*Pointing to a row of empty desks in the background*) But where are the feelings? (*pauses*) We have only eight bars to remember, because the last four are repeated. (*The memories are obviously interested; they like a piece to be short. Muscular Memory with his forceful glance gives a hint to his habits to get ready, but the conductor rebukes them*) I beg of you to relax until you are wanted. (*Pointing to Memories Aural and Muscular*) You will make a big crescendo up to bar 4. (*At this moment the feelings crowd into their places. Addressing them*) You are late again. (*The feelings look wan. The very thought of a clock puts them out. To the others*) After the climax there is a long diminuendo until the end. (*Tapping with his baton the time values of the first four beats*) This is the rhythmic pattern of every bar—very easy to remember. There is a little crescendo, too, at every third beat. (*The Sense of Time appears upset.*) So we have here an example of wrong barring. (*The memories replace the bar-lines at the third beat throughout.*) But for the sake of convenience we shall number the bars as they stand in the score. (*Glancing over the entire orchestra*) Now . . . all of you. (*They begin, but owing to a mistake of Visual Memory, some habits produce E natural.*) C minor, *please*. Key is a most important association. I want you to note the sequence in bar 2. This second phrase is in A flat major. The third returns to C minor; while the fourth modulates to the dominant. Some conductors allow an E natural throughout the third bar, but in Chopin's own edition the second E is flat. (*Visual Memory is overcome with surprise. Turning to Time*) I did not ask for a triplet at the third beat. It is TUM . . tee-tum. Time-names, please. (*Time recites 'ta-éfé taa' in a hollow voice. Addressing the fingering habits*) Change, please. (*After a whispered discussion with Muscular Memory, a few habits change places, where they appear more comfortable.*) Here is an interesting point. Let us play bar 2 . . . now bar 8. These begin the same way, but though bar 2 stays in A flat, bar 8 returns to the tonic. (*The memories make a note of this.*) In bar 7 you will find a first inversion of the tonic chord. (*The feelings are turning pale.*) Now, gentlemen (*every one sits up*), from the beginning. (*Music begins.*) I want the tone of an organ. . . . I cannot hear the bass. . . . I want a richer bass. (*Habits of arm weight respond, but those of pedalling lose their place. Covering his ears with his hands*) This cacophony is intolerable. (*To the pedalling habits*) You must practise in the interval. Until then, I ask you to keep quiet. (*To the others*) Once more, from the beginning . . . louder . . . louder; (*he appeals to the feelings*) give me all you can. (*The feelings glow rapturously.*) Magnificent! Now . . . soft . . . softer . . . softer still . . . the repeat (*with a glance at the delicate feelings*) like an echo. (*He pauses. Peremptorily*) Back to the beginning.

Enter the Habit of Mind-wandering

(*There is a sudden commotion in the orchestra.*) Gentlemen. (*The memories look vaguely at the habits. Rapping his baton*) Once more . . . from the beginning. . . . STOP! (*To the memories*) Muscular Memory is bars ahead. (*To the habits*) Some of you are behaving deplorably. Pedalling habits, please keep your feet still. I cannot hear myself think. (*To Mind-wandering*) What business have *you* to be here? You were banished long ago from the Union of Intelligent Practitioners. (*To the others*) Gentlemen, I beg of you. This is the hour for work. (*Looks round the orchestra appealingly. The memories are trying to be interested, but they are obviously tired. Many of the habits are already asleep. Throwing down his baton*) Interval! (*The conductor leaves the scene in a bad temper. The memories rehearse the pedalling habits for a few bars; then every one relaxes, while Mind-wandering amuses the orchestra with stories without end.*)

Curtain

Owing to lack of space, it is impossible to reproduce the remainder of this play, which consists of a thousand acts. Therefore, for the convenience of the student, the instructions of Intelligence are given below in condensed form. After following these in detail, every musician should be able successfully to direct his orchestra of memories and habits, however undisciplined they may at first appear.

E

III

CHAPTER XI

GENERAL RULES

1. Practise at regular hours.
2. Make the first impressions correct and musical.
3. When learning anything, concentrate on one point at a time.
4. Learn notes and chords in groups. Should you not know harmony, learn chords by shape—by the intervals they contain.
5. Choose a fingering that suits both your hand and the passage played; this fingering should not be altered.
6. Memorize expression just as carefully as notes.
7. Compare passages that resemble each other in any way.
8. Learn music, not bar by bar, but in phrases or longer musical divisions.
9. When revising, it is unnecessary to return to the beginning of a piece: the previous phrase will make a starting-point.
10. Use few repetitions at frequent intervals.
11. If a passage defeats you, leave it until another day.
12. Cultivate accuracy; facility will follow.
13. When a piece is becoming familiar, begin by rehearsing the most difficult portions.
14. Concentrate on improving one aspect of the music at a time—tone colour, legato, pedalling, &c.
15. After a mistake, go over the faulty passage once slowly; the last impression, like the first, should be correct.
16. In every piece practise beginning at prearranged 'headings'. (See para. 15, p. 53.)
17. Relax your mind, and allow movements to be subconscious.
18. Do not try to look ahead; rely on the contiguity of the music to suggest what is coming.
19. If you think you are going to forget, turn your attention to rhythm and expression.

20. Should you forget a passage when practising, look at the printed music immediately, and try to find the cause of the mistake. (See Rule 15.)

21. Should you forget when performing, and be unable to improvise, do not go back—go on to the musical heading that follows.

22. When mentally rehearsing music learnt, hear the sounds, but do not name the notes. Consciously think of the expression if you wish to improve this.

RULES FOR REPETITION

1. Repeat a passage only about three times in succession. Practise it thirty times in the day, if you like, dividing up the repetitions.

2. Between each repetition pause long enough to breathe.

3. Because the rate of conscious forgetting is most rapid in the case of new material, revise it frequently to begin with.

4. After some rehearsals, lay a piece away, making rest periods doubly long with increasing knowledge of the piece.

Suggested Scheme of Repetition

(To be adapted to suit the length and difficulty of any piece studied.)
Practice— 3 days (in succession)
Rest   — 3 „
Practice— 3 „
Rest   — 6 „
Practice— 3 „
Rest   —12 „
Practice— 2 days only, and so on.

Other pieces (preferably several) should be studied during periods marked 'rest'. Eventually a piece will require only an occasional rehearsal. (See para. 8, pp. 37–8.)

CHAPTER XII

LESSON 1

CHORDS

However advanced, students should read the following instructions carefully.

EXAMPLE 1—PRELUDE, OP. 28, NO. 7, BY CHOPIN

(1) Number the bars from the first complete bar.[1]

Part 1   bars 1 to 8 (2nd beat).
„   2   „   8 (3rd beat) to end.

(2) Every phrase is alike in time. Memorize the time pattern below. Read para. 4, p. 36.

Ex. *a.*

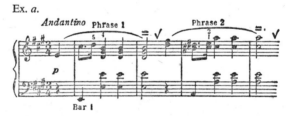

(3) Put a mark after every minim (half note); number each of the eight phrases accordingly.

(4) Examine and play each phrase, arranging fingering. See para. 6, p. 26; also pp. 108–9.

(5) Compare phrases 1 and 5; phrases 2 and 6. At 12 associate A sharp with the climax.

(6) Play the piece straight through once or twice slowly. See Rule 15.[2]

Second Rehearsal

(7) Repeat analysis of first rehearsal.

(8) Play each phrase, then the whole piece once or twice, playing less consciously than hitherto. Though looking at notes, give your attention to listening.

[1] Unless stated, numbers within paragraphs refer to the bars of the pieces given.
[2] Rules alluded to are those on pp. 50–1.

Third Rehearsal

(9) Once more revive conscious associations, noticing things first in L.H. then in R.H.[1] The progression of the bass is especially important. (Here the lowest notes are either E or A except at 13.) Never learn single notes; if necessary to think of notes, learn them by interval. See Rule 4.

(10) Relax your hands on your lap; shut your eyes, and think the first phrase. Rule 22.

(11) Play the first phrase from memory. You should feel as if your hands were moving about of their own accord. The less you look at the keyboard the better. With closed eyes you may mentally see keyboard or music, possibly both. Should you forget a passage, either you do not know it well enough, or you are consciously interfering with your memory. In the first case, give the habits further conscious help; in the second, repeat para. 10.

(12) Learn the second phrase in the same way; then play both from memory.

(13) Add phrase by phrase, linking each up with previous material. Rule 9.

(14) Play the whole piece through from memory; if necessary, once with the music. Rule 15.

15. *Headings*

Finally lay out the piece under headings, as you would a speech. These should be starting-points, or 'stations', in case of accident, and they are useless unless you can recall the music that follows. You may arrange a heading at the beginning of every phrase in a slow piece like this; and you should rehearse from memory all passages that resemble each other. (Play phrase 1, saying 'first time'; phrase 5, saying 'second time'. Rehearse phrases 2 and 6 in the same way.) Afterwards practise beginning at the headings in reverse order—at the last; at the last but one; at the one before that.

Headings should only be arranged at points that will not interrupt the musical line.

---

[1] It is customary to abbreviate the words 'right hand' and 'left hand' using the initials R.H. and L.H. respectively.

16. *Retention*

However easy a piece, it should be analysed more than once, and relearnt at close intervals. Whether or not you can play music after learning it once, you should go over the same ground *at least three times*. See Rule 3, p. 51.

OUTLINE OF METHOD

1. Conscious practice with music.
2. Subconscious performance with music.
3. Revival of conscious impressions with music.
4. Subconscious performance from memory.
5. Arrangement of headings in every piece, and practice beginning at different places.

In the case of a difficult piece, postpone stage 4 until the music is quite clear in the mind.

17. *Practice Hours*

First rehearsals are tiring, and a period of 15 or 20 minutes is long enough to give to the learning of new material; give the remainder of the hour to other music.

Suggestion for the Practice Hour

15 minutes—Memorizing of new piece.

    „   „   —Technical exercises for which difficult passages from pieces provide interesting material.

5   „   —Rest.

25 „   —Improvement of old pieces, including those memorized recently.

The number of hours to be given daily to musical work must be decided by the individual; a student with nothing to think of but music can naturally practise longer without fatigue than a teacher who gives most of his energy to the work of others. After a period without practice, one must get 'into training' gradually. See para. 8, pp. 37–8.

EXAMPLE 2—PRELUDE, OP. 16, NO. 3, BY SCRIABIN

(1) Play the melody and learn the fingering given in Ex. *b*, p. 109. The piece is built on this theme; fragments of it are to be found in the

chordal interludes. Compare theme beginning at 5, 11, and 24. (See footnote, p. 52.)

(2) Compare the R.H. part of these passages. Make them delicate and expressive.

(3) Noting modulations, play the rest of the piece as follows:

9 (2nd beat) to 11 (1st beat). Both hands together. Compare with

15 (2nd beat) to 17 (1st beat).

17 (,, ,,) ,, 18 (3rd beat). Compare with L.H. in 5; also with

20 (2nd beat) ,, 21 (3rd beat).

18 (4th ,,) ,, 20 (1st ,,). Compare with

21 (,, ,,) ,, 24 (,, ,,). Climax at 23.

28 (2nd ,,) ,, 30 (,, ,,). Breathe before repeating; breathe again and add

32 (2nd beat) to 33 (1st beat). Breathe and add final chords.

(4) Put the whole piece together. It should not sound 'straight', yet no beat should be cut short. Make a breath pause after every phrase mark.

(5) For further rehearsal, follow instructions given in previous lesson. See paras. 7–16, pp. 52–4.

EXAMPLE 3—CHORAL (FROM PRELUDE, CHORAL AND FUGUE)
BY CÉSAR FRANCK
(For advanced players only)

This part of the piece begins with the last bar of the Prelude, but number bar 1 after change of key-signature. (See footnote, p. 52.)

(1) 11 (4th beat) to 19 (3rd beat). By singing the melody you will find misplaced bar-lines; there are many throughout the piece. At first play the chords, leaving out arpeggios and upper octaves.

Ex. *b.*

Bar 11

Compare the whole passage with those beginning in 24 and 46, noting modulations. 15 (4th beat) to 19 (3rd beat) is repeated almost exactly in 50 to 54. This passage does not reappear at 28. Instead you will find another passage resembling that at 54 (4th beat).

(2) 1–11. Play bass and melody only; in the first four bars the accent is at 3rd beat. Though one long line, divide as follows:

1–5 (2nd beat). Note sequence.

5 (3rd beat) to 8 (1st beat). Sequence in L.H.

(3) 1–11. Play as written, very slowly, arranging fingering to suit legato. Pedal must not blur passing-notes.

(4) 19 (4th beat) to 24 (3rd beat). Practise as in paras. 2 and 3.

(5) 32 (,,   ,,) ,, 46 (,,   ,,). Practise as in para. 2; then divide as follows:

32 (4th beat) to 36 (3rd beat). Note sequence.

36 (,,   ,,) ,, 40 (,,   ,,). Note sequence and repetition.

40 (,,   ,,) ,, 43 (1st ,,). Repetition in bass.

43 (2nd ,,) ,, 46 (3rd ,,).

Practise the whole passage as in para. 3.

(6) This piece sounds most impressive when the bass moves strictly in time, except where marked. Though slight rubato may be felt in the melody, triplets should sound like triplets. Make every variety of tone colour. The top notes in the arpeggios should be softer than the octaves below. For further rehearsal carefully follow instructions given in paras. 7–16, pp. 52–4.

QUESTIONS ANSWERED

1. *Can one memorize music without a knowledge of harmony?*

Yes; but harmony provides so many musical associations that without it a student is greatly handicapped. For the purpose of learning, however, to know the name of a chord is less important than to understand its context.

2. *I have been told of the success of the 'whole' method of learning poetry. Should one ever learn a piece by repeating it from beginning to end without a break?*

Every piece contains portions more difficult than others, portions that require extra repetition. Besides, no player will feel confident who cannot begin at different points within a piece. See para. 15, p. 53.

3. *Is it advisable to read an easy piece completely before analysing it?*

It is better at first to take every piece in small portions: the quick reader will then let nothing pass unnoticed, while the slow reader, by simplifying the music, will understand it more clearly.

4. *Being able mentally to hear music I see, I have always learnt a piece away from the instrument. May I continue to do this?*

By all means, provided you give the muscular habits sufficient practice afterwards.

5. *Should one memorize the left hand alone?*

To do so is helpful in many passages, especially when the melody is in the bass, or if the bass is difficult. See, however, para. 2, p. 69.

6. *How soon should one play from memory?*

That depends on the piece and also on the quality of your memory. By the method given it is possible to play from memory at the first rehearsal, immediately after the required analysis; but those who do may be tempted to give too much attention to notes, and too little to expression.

7. *Though I know the first lesson perfectly, I cannot play it to any one without breaking down. What should I do?*

Go through the piece, bit by bit, with a friend beside you. Discuss a portion; then play it from memory, thus reducing the length of the memory test. By talking about the music, you will begin to lose self-consciousness. Finally, relax, and try to play the whole piece by heart.

8. *I have mapped out my piece as you suggest, but I cannot begin in the middle of a passage. Does this matter?*

Certainly not. Would the part of 'Hamlet' be easier to remember if one tried to begin in the middle of a word or phrase?

9. *What am I to do in the case of an old piece I have learnt in my own way?*

If you feel sure of it, do not pull it to bits; but arrange starting-points in every piece. See para. 15, p. 53. If any passage is not clear in your mind, analyse it carefully for three days running.

10. *I am a good improviser. Will this interfere with my memory?*

Not as long as you analyse music you learn. To be able to improvise will give you confidence when playing from memory, because, in case of a slip, you will be able to bridge a possible gap in the music.

11. *Should I give up sight-reading until I learn to play by heart?*

Practise sight-reading as much as you like, but do not read at sight superficially pieces you intend to play from memory.

12. *I cannot practise every day. Does this matter?*

Not if you practise well. Those who practise daily may do less than others who practise irregularly, but with more zest.

13. *I have no time for practice until evening, when I am tired. Must I give up all idea of learning new music?*

Certainly not; but never start work without having a short rest; then begin with the most difficult portions of your pieces.

14. *I find I do my best work at night. Must I make myself practise in the morning?*

Choose the hour that suits you best. Most people do their best conscious work in the morning; their practice of performance later in the day.

15. *Owing to recent illness I find my memory unreliable. Should I try to learn new music?*

Not unless you must; memory improves with health.

CHAPTER XIII

Lesson 2

BROKEN CHORDS

Example 1—Prelude, Book 1, No. 1, from Bach's '48'

(1) In learning a passage or piece composed of broken chords, it is best at first to play all the notes of each chord together. In this piece there is but one chord in each bar to remember.

Ex. *a.*

Bar 1

(2) Read para. 6, p. 45. By playing chords unbroken you will understand the shape of the piece, which can be divided into two parts:

Bars 1 to 19.

„ 20 „ 35.

(3) Playing one chord in each bar, divide the piece as follows:

1–4. Rules 4 and 5, p. 50.

5–11. Modulation to dominant. Note sequence.

12–13. Note modulation, and compare with

14–15.

16–19. Compare with 8–11.

(4) After 20, the bass is feeling its way to the dominant pedal at 24.[1] From here onwards is one line, but you may think of it in smaller portions:

24–27.

28–31.

32–35. Tonic pedal with passing modulation. In the last bars, notes comprising broken chords can be learnt in sets of three in R.H.

(5) Play the piece straight through exactly as written.

[1] In some editions an extra bar with a G bass is interpolated after 22. This extra bar is **not** included here; the bass of 23 is A flat.

Second Rehearsal

(6) Relearn the piece as at previous rehearsal.

(7) Still playing one chord in each bar, play each portion, and finally the whole piece from memory. See para. 11, p. 53; also Rule 9. In future always practise the piece as written. Read para. 15, p. 53.

EXAMPLE 2—FIRST MOVEMENT FROM BEETHOVEN'S 'MOONLIGHT' SONATA, OP. 27, NO. 2

(1) Block out the shape of the piece:

Introduction

A 1 Bars 5 (4th beat) to 28 (1st beat).
B   ,, 28 (2nd ,,) ,, 42 (3rd ,,).
A 2 ,, 42 (4th ,,) ,, 60 (,,   ,,).
Coda ,, 60 (,,   ,,) ,, 69.

(2) Leaving out the musical background, play bass and melody only. Read para. 6, p. 26. Noting modulations, subdivide the piece as follows:

1 to 5 (3rd beat).
5 (4th beat) to 10 (3rd beat).
10 (,,   ,,) ,, 15 (,,   ,,). Compare with previous phrase.

(3) 15 (,,   ,,) ,, 19 (2nd ,,). Another idea stated twice.
19 (3rd ,,) ,, 23 (3rd ,,).
23 (4th ,,) ,, 28 (1st ,,).

(4) 28 (2nd ,,) ,, 42 (3rd ,,). Continue to play bass and melody only. Note dominant pedal.

(5) 42 (4th beat) to 46 (3rd beat). Repetition of phrase at 5; but notice that phrase at 10 does not reappear.

(6) 46 (4th beat) to 51 (3rd beat). Compare with phrase beginning at 23.
51 (4th beat) to 55 (2nd beat). Compare with phrase at 16.
55 (3rd ,,) ,, 60 (3rd ,,).
60 (4th ,,) ,, end.

(7) Play the whole piece, keeping chords unbroken.

Ex. *b.*

(8) Broken chords usually lie under the hand in sets of three or four notes. Finger them accordingly, regardless of black keys. Those at 32 and 62 are most easily learnt thus:

Ex. *c.*

Ex. *d.*

(9) After going through the entire piece as suggested, play it once exactly as it is written. Rule 15.

Second Rehearsal

(10) The chief difficulty consists in keeping triplets in the background. See para. 7, p. 37; also Ex. *f,* p. 29. Practise the piece in musical sections both short and long, giving attention to playing the triplets evenly and softly. At 32 you have to learn to build up a climax without quickening the tempo perceptibly.

Third Rehearsal

(11) Take phrase by phrase as at the first rehearsal, playing the notes of each beat as one chord. You may then play each phrase from memory in the same way, linking it up with previous material. Rule 9. Carefully read paras. 7–16, pp. 52–4. In future play the piece as it is written.

DETAILED MUSIC

1. *What is Detail?*

IN some music it is difficult to see the wood for the trees, and one should begin by eliminating what may obscure the view of essentials. Any moving part has obviously more to say than a part that is stationary; and the passage at bar 9 of the last movement of Beethoven's 'Moonlight' Sonata is given here with upper part left out. The theme should be considered before possible technical difficulties.

Ex. *a*. Beethoven, Op. 27, No. **2.**

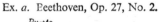

See also Ex. *k*, p. 30.

2. *Time and Ornament*

Ornaments are better omitted until the notes they ornament are in their right place. A trill, for example, is never meant to interrupt the time, and in the following, shakes have purposely been omitted. Compare with original (Nocturne, No. 5).

Ex. *b*. Chopin, Op. 15, No. **2.**

After feeling the melodic line, no student will ask the question, 'How many notes should I put into a shake?' Time alone can decide.

3. *Patterns*

After sketching the musical outline, play an ornamental passage very slowly, giving attention to its construction. There is nearly always a pattern (or patterns) to remember, and the first bar of the passage (above) can be learnt thus:

a. Chromatic sixths, fingered accordingly.
b. Chromatic scale.
c. Notes encircling E sharp.
d. Melodic link leading to next bar.

In the fourth bar (at *e*) there are only two sets of notes to remember; and when choosing fingering, play each set as in Lesson 2.

4. *First Impressions*

The student may say, 'Since the first impression is so important, may I not learn the piece wrongly by leaving out some parts of it?' This is unlikely, because, seeing detail, one knows it is there. In any case the suggested procedure is safer than that followed by many students who practise a piece, hoping to find out eventually what it is all about. In the meantime the music may be distorted; background becomes foreground; wrong habits of expression creep in—habits difficult to change. The temporary omission of less important parts is suggested merely as a preliminary to learning, when, before allowing his fingers to perform a passage, the student asks himself, 'What is it that I want my fingers to do?' The division of parts described on p. 35 will greatly help in the study of detailed music, because it makes clear what is bass, what is melody, and what is merely ornamentation.

5. *Rapid Music*

The quicker the piece, the more important becomes the right stressing of bars. Chopin's Scherzo in B minor, for instance, is extremely difficult to play if accented wrongly; but when bars are stressed musically (in this case, alternately strong and weak) the piece becomes comparatively easy to play. See para. 4, p. 36.

Though more difficult technically, quick music is much easier to perform from memory than slow: movements are so closely associated that muscular memory may be capable of learning a piece without even the assistance of aural memory. But the player who learns in this way knows in his heart that he is but half-prepared; and to feel sure of oneself in any piece, one must understand to begin with what is taking place in the music. Therefore, even the skilled student should analyse rapid music at the first rehearsals with just as much care as slow music; he will then be able to dispense with much detailed analysis at later rehearsals. In fact, when one reaches the stage of final analysis preparatory to memory-playing, it is unnecessary to analyse everything consciously (as is occasionally necessary in music that is very slow); much can be left to memories aural and muscular. It is usually enough at the end to learn consciously only outstanding features of the music, such as the movement of the bass.

6. *Headings*

All proficient musicians rely much on muscular memory in the performance of rapid music; and because it is inadvisable to break up unnecessarily the chains of thought upon which muscular memory depends, one should arrange far fewer headings in rapid music than in music that is very slow. And, as there is less danger of forgetting the former, fewer starting-points are necessary.

SUMMARY
1. Conscious analysis (very detailed) with music.
2. Subconscious performance with music.
3. Conscious analysis (less detailed) with music.
4. Subconscious performance from memory.

7. *Independent Time*

Two notes to a beat in one part against three in another part can be learnt by means of the time-names 'ta-téfé-ti';

　sounds the same as

But with varied groups it is impossible to count the subdivisions of independent parts in combination; and it is useless to try to dovetail them, because they will be independent no longer. The only way to play such music artistically is to start the hands together, and allow each to go its own way until they arrive together on the required beat. In such music it is wise to perfect each part alone; then the player who has learnt to relax his mind will have little difficulty with it, though a certain amount of practice is necessary in order to remember the sensation of independent part-playing. Needless to say, it is impossible to follow two (or more) combined parts with equal attention; one or other has to be relegated to a great extent to memories tactual and muscular.

8. *Habits of Touch*

However consciously rapid music is learnt, however slowly, it should never be practised too heavily, else wrong technical habits will form. A passage played slowly feels different from the same passage played quickly; and to be able to think a passage is not enough: in the end, one is obliged to play very rapid music partly through muscular sensation. There is a 'knack' of playing each passage, and that knack must be found in practice and remembered for future use. To rehearse a passage sometimes on the surface of the keys (without sounding notes) will help the student to remember the sensations of playing with little or no arm weight.

EXAMPLE 1—PRELUDE, BOOK 1, NO. 3, FROM BACH'S '48'

(1) When rhythmical patterns are understood, this piece becomes less difficult than it looks. Play the passage at 6; without breaking legato, mentally group notes according to dotted lines. (Alternatives are given.)

Ex. *c.*

See para. 8, p. 67; also para. 4, p. 36. In this piece bars are alternately strong and weak until the final cadence.

(2) Play the passages that resemble the above, now beginning at

(R.H.)	22	(L.H.)	14
	35		30
	43		39
			52

Mentally group these patterns alike, noting sequences; and arrange a comfortable fingering for each section in relation to what precedes and follows. The section at 14, for instance, should be physically connected both with the end of 13 and the beginning of 17.

(3) Beats must not be disconnected unless marked. See Ex. *k*, p. 30.

(4) Play R.H. and L.H. separately from 25 to 47. Mentally join each tied note to following note.

Ex. *d.*

Bar 35

(5) Broken chords 1–5, 9–13, &c., may be learnt according to Lesson 2; also those from 63 onwards.

(6) Noting modulations subdivide the piece as follows:

1–9 (1st note).

9–17 (,,). Compare with previous section. Because one section ends where the next begins, you may start each section on the beat.

17–25 (1st note). Compare with first section.

25–35 (,,). Compare with 9–17. The change at 32 is important.

35–39 (1st note). Compare with previous section.

39–43 (,,).   ,,   ,,   ,,   ,,

43–47 (,,).

47–55 (,,). Same as 9–17 in F sharp.

55–63 (,,). Compare with first section.

63–75 (,,). Play one chord in each bar. Note dominant pedal.

75–87 (1st note). Note sequence.

87–97 („). Play one chord in each bar. Note dominant pedal.

97 to end. Dominant bass continues.

(7) As the parts are of equal importance, each may be rehearsed separately. Carefully read para. 2, p. 69.

(8) To ensure rhythmical playing, it is helpful in the early stage to linger slightly on the first note of each bar, without breaking the musical line. This ensures also that both hands arrive together on the beat.

EXAMPLE 2—STUDY, OP. 25, NO. 9, BY CHOPIN

(1) Many people find this piece difficult because they stress the music according to the bar-lines, misplaced as far as 32. If you play the melody with the thumb, you will hear that the real stress is at the second beat, with cadence at 8 (beat 2). Bar-lines at 37 onwards clearly give the key to the rhythm of the beginning.

(2) Divide the piece as follows:

Bars 1–8.

9–16.

17–25 (1st note).

25–37 („) followed by coda.

(3) 1–4. Note descending bass. Compare pattern with

5–8.

9–12. Compare with

13–16.

17–20. Compare with

21–24.

25–28. Compare with first phrase.

29–37. The melody may be played (by the thumb) along with the bass, which is easy to remember. C natural in L.H. is the signal for the climax. Compare 29–30 with 5–6.

37–51. Compare the patterns in R.H. and note change of pitch at 41.

(4) Practise the piece also in the longer sections given in para. 2. Read para. 6, p. 64; also 'Technique', p. 108.

CHAPTER XV

LESSON 4

CONTRAPUNTAL MUSIC

MUSIC consisting of two or more moving parts is the most difficult kind of music to remember; therefore, those who have played little from memory are advised not to attempt fugue without preparation. After learning some music of the types of the earlier lessons, the student should memorize some of Bach's very simple pieces, to be followed by the easier two-part Inventions.

1. *Difficulties of Part-playing*

In para. 7, p. 65, it was stated that it is not difficult for the technically proficient to play independent parts simultaneously; but in contrapuntal music the parts are interdependent; hence attention seems divided. In reality, attention moves quickly from part to part, now accentuating an entry, now subordinating one part to another. To perform as freely as this, one requires a thorough knowledge of what is taking place in the music as well as the ability to switch attention from part to part without interfering with habits of technique. Though very few musicians find this type of music easy to play from memory, performance can be rendered less difficult by postponing it until the player clearly knows what he intends to do with the musical lines, and until the habits of expression are ready to perform semi-consciously.

It would be well for pianists to remind themselves that parts in contrapuntal music are 'voices'. Now in piano-playing a note cannot 'sing' for long without sufficient initial tone; therefore, melodic notes require tone in proportion to their duration. In Ex. *d*, p. 66, the tied notes are obviously meant to be emphatic, and they require more tone than others if they are to last for two beats.

Below is another example showing the need for variation of tone quantity in relation to the length of the note played. Suspensions lose their meaning if their connexion with the following notes is inaudible.

Ex. *a.* Bach, Prelude, Bk. 1, No. 16.

Lento moderato

Many examples from Bach have already been given, and so much stress has been laid on the importance of rhythmical and musical thinking that here it is enough to remind the student that he should mentally group and 'think' every line of notes while learning them. Later on, the habits of expression can be entrusted with the parts that are temporarily of lesser importance in the musical scheme.

2. *Method of Procedure*

(1) Take each voice by itself; sing it, phrase it, sketch the colouring (the expression). You may practise each part separately but not too much; if you do, if you learn separate parts from memory, you will probably have to re-learn them when co-ordinating the habits. After the preliminary study of separate parts advised in para. 3, p. 35, it is important to adhere to the fingering you will use when the piece is completed.

(2) Put all the parts together, concentrating temporarily on fingering.

(3) Play the entire piece very slowly indeed, giving attention to the bass, while following it mentally throughout. Play the piece again, this time following the tenor voice; and twice more when there are two upper parts to consider. (The same musical idea should be phrased in the same way in whichever part it appears.)

(4) Make up your mind about the relative importance of the parts, and arrange tone-colour accordingly. (Where the organist would change registration the pianist should alter touch.) Give due attention also to important points, such as entries.

(5) Though it is advisable to arrange a few starting-points in every piece, the music should not be broken up at the wrong place. For

instance, should one sentence end on a strong beat, the heading should be arranged after that beat, not on it.

3. *Memory-playing*

Do not attempt to lay the music aside until you begin to feel that your fingers, as well as your mind, know the music. Even at this stage it is usually advisable to give further conscious rehearsal to ensure success. You will find some passages harder to remember than others; and in a difficult case it is helpful to analyse the chords occurring on each beat, and to associate other notes of the passage with these 'skeleton' chords. Read Rule 20. After extra practice of any portion, it should be linked up with others before and after: no passage should be disassociated for long from its surroundings.

4. *Back to Consciousness*

Any one who cannot differentiate between a harmony and a passing-note will find it difficult to pick out essentials; and it can now be understood how valuable is a knowledge of harmony to the learner. Much will be missed, too, without an intellectual appreciation of fugue. Understanding musicians find delight in beautiful devices that the un-initiated rarely notice—imitation, inversion, stretto—devices that can make the study of this music enthrallingly interesting; and an appreciation of which greatly simplifies the learning, not only of all contrapuntal music, but of every other kind of music as well.

Example 1—Two-Part Invention in F major, No. 8, by Bach

(1) The first part of this piece is a canon—one part follows another, saying precisely the same thing. L.H. repeats R.H. (a bar later) as far as 8, where the exact imitation ceases.

At 12, L.H. states the first idea, now followed by R.H., but at 15 the latter introduces a new figure, and from now onwards the canon is not complete; but you should notice how the parts imitate each other in many places. The R.H. part from 13 to 15 is imitated in G minor by L.H. in 17–19; and in 21 (L.H.) you will find a hint of the first idea, the music now descending for a change. 29–34 is a transposition of 8–12.

(2) Play R.H. alone as follows:

1 to 3 (1st note).

3 (2nd note) to 7 (1st note).

7 („   ) „ 12.

(3) Play L.H. part as far as 12.

(4) Play L.H. alone as follows:

12–17 (1st note).

17 (2nd note) to 24 (1st note).

24 („   ) „ 30 („   ).

30 („   ) „ 34.

(5) 13–34. Practise R.H. likewise in musical sections.

(6) Play each hand alone from beginning to end, arranging fingering to suit phrasing. Read para. 2, p. 69.

(7) Put the parts together, playing very slowly. Read para. 8, p. 67.

(8) A piece like this should not be practised in small sections because the end of one section rarely coincides with that in the other part. A musical starting-point can be found at 12 (L.H. entry); and if others are necessary, arrange one at 16 (2nd quaver, or 8th note); another after the first note of 26.

(9) In the opening part of this chapter you will find instructions for the next rehearsals.

Example 2—Fugue, Book 1, No. 3, from Bach's '48'

(1) Mark with a pencil the entries of the subject (nearly all complete) at 1, 3, 5, 10, 14, 19, 24–8, 42, 44, 46, 52; you will find portions of it at 23, 24, 35, &c. The figure at 4 occurs frequently throughout the piece, sometimes inverted as in 7 and 31.

(2) Study each part in turn; note modulations and sketch the phrasing. See para. 2, p. 34.

(3) Those with keen aural memory may play one part and sing another against it. For others the method used in para. 3, p. 35, is easier.

(4) If you like, you may draw a plan of the fugue thus: on pages of music-paper the same size as your printed copy, draw bar-lines to correspond with the original ones, and in the same position. Do not write the notes; merely sketch the fugue's outline on the staves, by marking

where the entries take place and the parts in which they occur; mark also changes of key, climax, and so on. This suggestion corresponds with that given in para. 16, p. 96. Read also para. 2, p. 69.

(5) After preliminary practice, play the parts together, arranging fingering once and for all.

(6) Practice sections should not be too short. At 14 one may pause (though not on a passing-note). Another break can be made after the third beat of 22, the cadence chord. That the bar-line is misplaced is proved by the fact that entries of the subject from here onwards to 42 are differently barred from those in the exposition. The player who stresses the middle portion of the fugue according to the bar-lines given will possibly have difficulty in playing it from memory later on. Thus we re-learn our first lesson—that the presence of Intelligence is essential at the preliminary rehearsal of every kind of music, including Fugue.

ADDITIONAL SUGGESTIONS

1. *Music of Different Types*

A piece usually contains more than one type of music, and the various ideas given may be applied to different portions or passages of any piece, according to their type. For example, the third movement from Beethoven's Sonata, Op. 31, No. 3, may be studied, at first, as suggested in para. 3, p. 35.

Ex. *b*. Beethoven, Op. 31, No. 3.

This and the Trio can be memorized according to Lesson 1; the few broken chords treated as shown in Lesson 2.

2. *Sonatas and Long Pieces*

It is possible to be discouraged by the look of a long piece, but sometimes the task appears more formidable than need be. The usual procedure is to start at the beginning, learning a page or two at a time; but to do this gives undue emphasis to the beginning. The beginning is easy to remember, because, being new, it arrests attention; the end is easy to remember, because the work is nearly done; it is the middle portion of any long task (like the afternoon task of the factory worker) that is the most irksome, because there seems so much to get through. The mind is naturally lazy, and Intelligence should lay out a musical task so that it appears neither boring nor too difficult. Below are three points specially applicable to the learning of long pieces:

(1) Preliminary survey of the movement from beginning to end.
(2) Detailed study and comparison of all passages that resemble one another, followed by occasional practice of the piece as a whole.
(3) Special study of difficult portions.

In this way are combined methods 'whole' and 'partial'; and it will be found that by putting side by side all the appearances of each subject, by comparing them, along with their 'bridge' passages, the piece will quickly take shape in the mind. A development section is not postponed; at first sight one searches in it for principal subjects, probably altered and disguised by the device of the composer, and passing through the adventures of many tonalities. Of course, it is much easier not to think; it is much easier not to turn back the music pages and compare recapitulation with exposition, coda with development; but memorizing is thinking, and no good musician can dispense with it. The student is not unrewarded: a long piece appears less long, and a practice hour becomes all too short for the discovery of the many interesting things hidden in every well-written sonata, classical or modern.

3. *Division of Work*

The student may say, 'If I am to give only twenty minutes at a time to the memorizing of a piece, how am I ever to learn a whole sonata?' To learn a little thoroughly is better than to learn a great deal superficially; and for the final memorizing preparatory to memory-playing, the work may be laid out something like this:

3 days—memorizing of all appearances of first subject.
   ,, —memorizing of all appearances of second subject.
   ,, —memorizing of bridge passages.
   ,, —special work on development section.

After the first minutes of concentrated work the player may run through material previously learnt, occasionally playing (or silently reading) the piece from beginning to end; but it should be realized that passages thoroughly learnt are improved by an occasional rest. See p. 51. When an intelligent scheme takes the place of haphazard practice, it will be found that a long movement can be played from memory after a fortnight (possibly much less), provided that the preliminary study has been conscientious and artistic.

4. *Arrangement of Work*

The writer is frequently asked the question, 'How many pieces should I memorize at once?' On p. 51 it was suggested that work is rendered varied and interesting by the practice of many pieces. It does not seem to matter how many are studied—and, of course, all study worthy of the name is memory work—but in the writer's opinion the most satisfactory results are obtained by deciding which of the pieces practised is to be finally memorized and added to the memory repertoire, and that the first part of each day's practice be given to this piece until the student feels sure of it. Success hastens the speed of learning, and one who can play a few pieces from memory with certainty and authority will make more future progress than another who performs a great many, but none with confidence. If, however, it is found that a piece chosen is not yet ready to be played from memory, it should be temporarily laid aside, or relegated to the latter part of the practice hour, and another piece given the first place. Attention is keenest at the beginning of the rehearsal, and the first fifteen minutes are so valuable that they should be used to the greatest advantage.

CHAPTER XVI

LESSON 5

MODERN MUSIC

MODERN music ought to be easier to remember than classical, firstly, because it is more difficult to read; secondly, because unusual discords arrest attention. But, on the contrary, many people complain that they find modern music difficult to memorize, and for this there must be a reason. Now to remember any music with certainty one must study it with care and also enjoy it. But do even advanced players always study modern music as carefully as they do the classics? Some appear content merely to play the notes they see, creating a musical picture both distorted in outline and crude in colour—a picture that is pleasing to neither performer nor listener. There is an unfortunate belief that music tells its own story; but it does nothing of the kind: it tells the story of the interpreter; and the best modern music, like Bach, can sound meaningless if performed without understanding.

1. *Modern Types*

Music is of many types, and as every musician has a natural bent for certain kinds of music, in choosing his concert repertoire the performer should confine himself to pieces that suit his temperament, because these are the pieces he will learn most easily and also play the best. This applies also to the learning of modern music, where may be found, as well as atonality for the ultra-modern, melodies beautiful enough to satisfy the most romantic.

Modern music divides itself into two main types—music clear in outline and music nebulous. But even if the composer dispenses with barlines he cannot dispense with accent; he has necessarily to put his music into some sort of shape, and if the shape is significant, the content has the possibility of being good music. Within this shape will be found musical ideas, and the treatment of these, even more than the ideas themselves, will display the composer's greatness. Some modern music, however, is not well written; ideas follow without logical sequence, and this kind of music is as difficult to remember as a badly written dialogue for the film. But when the music is good, one idea leads to another with a musical reason, and it can be learnt in exactly the same way as classical music—by intelligent association.

2. *Idiom*

The idiom of Beethoven is so familiar that it has become our own language; and when we come across new ways of stating musical thought, we should not condemn them merely because we do not understand them at first sight. If we do, we shall miss much music that is not only interesting, but extremely beautiful to an ear accustomed to the unexpected. And if one patiently studies a new composer, one finds that he, like the writer of books, not infrequently repeats himself; he uses the same chords, the same devices, in various ways; and when one becomes accustomed to a new composer's style, each subsequent piece of his becomes easier to learn.

3. *A Modern Example*

The student must also bear in mind that because the notation of music has not been simplified with the teaching of it, he must expect much in modern music that is confusing, including misleading phrase-marks and bar-lines; and on a staff black with accidentals it is not always easy to trace the composer's thought. In the following example, are the bar-lines in the right place? Surely there ought to be one before the third beat of the second bar—the point to which the phrase leads up.

Ex. *a.* Prokofief, Op. 3, No. 3.

Allegro energico

After this it is encouraging to see a bass childishly easy to remember, because descending by semitone; and in the treble we find a sequence, which is always helpful. Can we discover any connexion between the chords? Picking out the first five accented chords, we make another chromatic progression to which can be attached the chords forming prefixes.

And in the second bar we come upon an augmented triad that gives us such a delightful surprise that we cannot help remembering it. So on throughout the piece, clearly and classically ternary in shape.

4. *Classical Devices*

In all modern music we find the devices of past composers, including imitations and sequences; and we should conscientiously search for such aids to memory. In so doing we discover other interesting things, which may give the key to the interpretation. Turn to Scriabin's Poem, Op. 32, No. 1, where, at the twenty-fifth bar, is a passage that appears highly complicated. But if you take the trouble to disentangle the two melodies from the background and compare this passage with the first bars, you will realize that nothing more unusual has happened than that the melody at first below has been transferred to the upper part.

Should any student find it hard to believe that much modern music is firmly rooted in the classics, let him compare two examples given in this book—Ex. *a*, p. 69, and Ex. *d*, p. 36. Here are two passages so alike that it is hard to believe that one was written by Bach, the other by Debussy. These passages so similar call for similar treatment—the same legato with careful fingering, the same beauty of expression. No more need be said, nor can be said. The only way to learn any music rightly is to love it enough to think about it.

5. *Problems of Development*

Although Intelligence can remove many technical difficulties and simplify the learning of music, every student must be prepared for other problems that will arise in the course of his development. Progress is never uninterrupted; after a period of improvement there will be a period when little or no improvement is apparent. But though the learner may then believe that he is crossing a mental desert, such experience is rarely barren: it is at these times that the inner mind is thinking over new material, co-ordinating and perfecting the habits preparatory to attaining another and higher level of achievement.

Serious students must also realize that, though there are legitimate 'short cuts' for the learner, there can be none for the interpreter: the greater an artist, the farther he has to go. But need a student go so far before becoming an artist? May not every intelligent child learn to find for himself more on a music page than mere notes? I hope that these chapters will enable the student to clear away some of the confusion created by music's notation, so that he, like an artist, may experience the joy of searching for the elusive spirit living in familiar symbols. Then music, like memory, will seem ever more mysterious, for in it is to be found, not one spirit, but countless spirits, whose message will sound meaningless, banal, ecstatic, according to the quality of the mind that interprets it. This is the last thing taught in the study of music; perhaps it should be the first.

IV

CHAPTER XVII

THE TEACHER

IMPORTANT as is the lesson hour, even more important are the hours spent by a pupil alone with his music. But even adults may waste time through unintelligent practice, and it is hardly fair to expect young people to know by instinct how to work; there are few pupils of any age who will not benefit by help in this direction. The teacher of to-morrow will be forced to consider this question of practice; with the crowded school curriculum it is becoming ever more necessary to find a method of work that will give good results with a minimum of time. Fortunately, short periods of musical practice can be very profitable.

In one school, where only as much time could be given to music as to any other subject, it was found by a visiting teacher that pupils made better progress than in another school where more time was available. Those having only short practice periods were apparently stimulated by having to find out how much they could do in a little time—on one day as little as ten minutes.

1. *Musical Instruments*

Every student remembers best what he most enjoys; but how can any one with a sensitive ear enjoy practice on some of the pianos at present provided in schools? Bad pianos both encourage mind-wandering and discourage musical appreciation; and it is the teacher's duty to urge parents and heads of schools to provide instruments in every sense musical. The full keyboard is the best for practice; otherwise, if a pupil becomes used to a shorter one, visual memory may be upset at a concert or examination.

2. *Practice*

Some parents (like some teachers of the past) believe that the quantity of work is more important than its quality; and these are partly responsible for the fact that many potential music-lovers, disheartened

79

by the boredom of so-called 'practice', give up 'taking music', usually to their deep regret in after-life. Teachers should seek the co-operation of parents, who sometimes require instruction as much as their children concerning practice.

A beginner's work should be supervised, preferably by some one who has attended the lesson; but if supervision cannot be arranged, teachers should not allow children to work alone until they learn how to make use of their time; and all young pupils could profit by a few preliminary practice lessons in classes assembled according to age and intelligence. Most children will take up with zest any idea which appeals either to their imagination or to their self-interest; and that time can be saved by methodical practice will appeal especially to the modern child, who already has so much to get through.

3. *Collecting Memories*

The writer has discovered by experience that even little children can be greatly interested and stimulated by a talk on memory. Two different photographs taken on one negative can be used to suggest the mental effect of playing a musical passage in two different ways—an illustration that emphasizes the importance of making accurate memory records. To one who collects stamps it is easy to bring home the result of interest and concentration. The child will readily understand that he remembers his stamps—their colour, shape, and design—through examining them minutely; comparison of one stamp with another further helps to fix them in the memory; and by looking at them again and again, the pictures become more and more clearly engraved in the mind.

Any normal child can learn to differentiate between actions performed consciously, and others, like habits, performed without thinking; yet it must be understood that every movement in playing (even if sub-conscious) is the result of a message from the brain. (It is a mistaken idea that such movements become 'reflex'.) Reasons for repetition should be given; and young people can be helped to realize the importance of the type of repetition employed, by means of fanciful illustrations.

(1) Chains of thought broken by a stop at an unmusical point.

(2) Mental knots caused by 'stammering'—the unnecessary (usually involuntary) repetition of notes.

(3) Unbroken chains of thought formed when playing without interruption.

Because most young music students want to run before they can walk, they must be convinced of the advantages to be gained from preliminary slow practice: when provided with a good reason for any rule given, children co-operate with their teacher far more readily.

The mind of a small child works less consciously than that of an older person, and no beginner should be worried by too much analysis; yet even the youngest can be led to notice things in music—form, changes of tonality, intervals, cadences perfect and imperfect, endings strong and weak. Such things (including the importance of expression) can well be taught in class, even by the 'private' teacher, who would thus be saved having to go over the same ground with every pupil in turn.

4. *The New Piece*

Without preliminary help, even a well-trained pupil may read a new piece wrongly; and teacher and pupil should discuss new material together before possible mistakes are memorized. At this preliminary practice, difficulties of time should be smoothed out, phrase marks added or altered, and a suitable fingering decided upon. In making these arrangements, of course, the pupil must have a say; but he must promise not to attempt to perform the piece as a whole until separate parts can be played correctly and musically. A teacher must always bear in mind that, as music was chosen by him as a career, he had a natural talent enabling him in youth to surmount many difficulties with comparative ease—difficulties that to others less gifted may seem prodigious. It is his duty, therefore, to present one point at a time, and to make his pupil think about it. Now that is the last thing the average

G

pupil wants to do; even adults will rarely take the trouble to learn correctly a passage like the following:

Ex. *a.* Chopin, Op. 15, No. 3.

As written, the parts are confusing to the eye; but made into a duet they at once become understandable.

Ex. *b.*

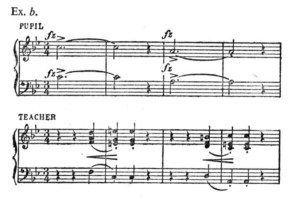

When technical difficulty is removed, the pupil can concentrate on the tone of each octave, which, orchestrated, might be played by trumpets. The chords, because 'saying' something different, might be allotted to strings; and on the piano these parts should differ in sonority. Teacher and pupil now change places (the latter playing the chords), and after hearing the musical effect it is comparatively easy to choose a fingering that will sustain long notes and also agree with given slurs. Who would wish to over-pedal this passage after hearing the long notes 'shining through' the chords? If the sense of any passage is clearly understood, everything becomes easier both to play and remember. (See also para. 3, p. 35.)

5. *Remembering a Tune*

In the case of any pupil who cannot easily recall a tune, memory for time should be developed apart from that of pitch—the first by means of French time-names; the second by means of hand-signs and sol-fa. This allows the learner to master difficulties separately: only when he can easily recall either pitch or time values is he ready to undertake the double task of recalling pitch in relation to time. To make the eye accurate, dictation is necessary, after which no learner will make the mistake of putting an accidental after a note, as even rapid sight-readers may do who have never examined music they play.

6. *Taste and Association*

Hand-signs and sol-fa are invaluable aids to memory, because they associate pitch and time with physical movements; but unnecessary associations, like far-fetched mnemonics, are undesirable. The linking of a verse with notes can certainly help the beginner to understand phrasing, but to associate ridiculous words with noble music (as is sometimes done in the teaching of Bach) is greatly to be deprecated. Individuals think of music in individual ways; and whatever associations the teacher may have with a piece, his pupils should be left free to form their own according to temperament. Some naturally link music with colour (a faculty called 'chromaesthesia'); others see music in patterns; but in order to appreciate or remember music it is not necessary to connect with it either story or picture. Form, however, is an integral part of music, and any pupil who tries to draw the curves that musical phrases suggest to him will find it easier both to interpret and remember them.

Some modern composers seem to believe that to attract a child music must be happy in mood and embellished with pictures and verses. But children differ in taste; many prefer sad music (as did the author of this book, who strongly disliked G major); others like their piece to be plain and 'grown-up' in appearance. A child should be given a choice of music: all people, young or not, play best and remember best music they like.

7. *From Memory*

When a pupil knows a piece he will tend to look away from the printed page. At this stage small children may usually play by heart quite safely; unless upset by other people, they will instinctively trust their memory. Older pupils, because more self-conscious, require more conscious support; and any intelligent child of fourteen (possibly less) can learn pieces exactly as suggested in Part III. All players, however young, should rehearse their music, beginning at prearranged 'headings'. Children like the idea of musical 'stations', and a 'junction' can be useful at any point where the music branches off.

To form a habit of playing before others is, of course, a necessity. Even if a teacher likes to give all lessons privately, rather than in class (as many of the greatest have done), he should never omit the private concert, the regular gathering of pupils for test performance, which should be part of the plan of every one who wishes pupils to do themselves and their music justice in public.

8. *Memory Games*

The young art student of to-day is trained to see and to remember. Why should not the student of music also have such training? This can be provided in the form of games as entertaining as profitable.

(1) The child is given a set period of time (say three minutes) to look at a number of objects collected together; afterwards he makes a list of all he can remember. This kind of practice can take place at odd minutes —before a shop-window, perhaps. Too many things should not be presented to the eye; at a museum, one case will provide plenty of material.

(2) (Game for two or more.) Spread out a pack of cards, face downwards; these must not overlap, and should not be arranged in any order. The first player takes up one card, which is looked at by both players, then laid down in exactly the same position as before, face downwards. The second player turns up another card (any he likes), which after being looked at by both players is replaced. The test of this game is in remembering the cards according to position. When, during the turn of either player, a pair can be made (two kings, for example), that player picks up the corresponding card (if he can remember exactly where it lies), putting the paired cards aside. He has then the right to take up another new card and make a second pair, if he can; possibly more. When the complete pack is paired off, the player who has found the most pairs is the winner. Complete silence must be observed during this game,

which, though requiring intense concentration, is much enjoyed by even small children.

In both these games, either card or article will be most easily remembered in relation to others—a king and a ten, for instance, can be more readily found if side by side—and by mentally going over the cards (or articles) several times the child recalls them more easily. Such games, therefore, not only induce spontaneous attention; they teach also the value of association and repetition. Neither game should be repeated often without a rest: the first of a series leaves such a vivid impression that visual memory becomes confused by different arrangements of either cards or articles. These games, then, can bring home to young people one of the most important things in the learning of everything, including music—the clarity of first impressions made with complete attention.

CHAPTER XVIII

THE ORGANIST

OWING to the lack of standardization of organs, the difficulties of playing without notes are very great for the organist. Variation of touch is, perhaps, the least of these difficulties: instruments differ in registration, in the number of manuals, in the gauge and possibly the weight of pedals. They differ, too, in response, which means that an organist's fingers may be ahead of the music that reaches his ears; and, to make matters yet more difficult, a performer may have but a short time in which to get accustomed to an instrument new to him.

An experienced organist, however, is usually a cultivated musician who, out of necessity, has learnt to improvise; and it is this practical knowledge of harmony that enables his memories to adapt themselves to unexpected conditions. In spite of obstacles that would seem insurmountable to some pianists, organists are playing more from memory than ever before, and not without reason.

1. *Advantages of Freedom*

Many church organists speak of the advantage of being able to play entirely from memory certain parts of the services, and to do this should be possible for any one who plays week after week on the same instrument. Every organist is hampered by having to keep eyes upon the music: registration has to be considered, also the turning of pages at convenient places. In the case of an unfamiliar instrument, the advantages of memory-playing are obvious. During performance with conducted choir or orchestra, the organist must necessarily watch the conductor's beat; and the recitalist who can play at least the first piece from memory has the best opportunity of becoming acquainted with an organ new to him. Therefore, though few busy organists can find time to memorize their complete repertoire, every one should learn by heart at least a few pieces. From the public's point of view the psychological effect of memory-playing has already been alluded to.

2. *Piano Practice*

Because piano study teaches technical fluency and correctness of fingering, a good pianist can now learn organ touch with a facility formerly denied him. Only when finger technique has become second nature can the organist's attention be free to express music by means of registration and that indefinable rubato, which, guided by feeling and taste, constitute 'style'.

Is it advisable for students to memorize organ music on a piano? Not without the necessary pedal attachment. Where the mistake is made of learning music of two staves, adding pedals as an afterthought, the player will have to re-learn a piece when co-ordinating the habits. It is certainly advisable to study any music in detail, and to perfect pedalling habits by temporarily giving them complete attention; but because the player's aim is to 'think' with feet and hands in combination, he must practise them together to make the necessary co-ordination subconscious.

3. *Useful Habits*

For students at home the following hints will prove helpful:

(1) Pieces of white paper may be affixed to the front of a piano, in the exact position of the pistons. These dummies should be touched when the pistons they represent would be required in organ-playing.

(2) Charts of the stops can be made on paper and hung up beside the piano. One should then arrange exact points in any piece at which the hands are to leave the manuals; and to render registration semiconscious one can practise silent registration, touching the dumb stops when required.

(3) The position of the pedals should be learnt through tactual and muscular memory. For example, if middle E flat is felt with the side of either foot, this pedal can be used as a gauge for others in its vicinity.

(4) Intervals can be gauged (at first consciously) by corresponding movements. In an arpeggio, for example, to cross the legs at the ankles will approximately correspond with the interval of a third; to cross them at the calf will suggest a fourth. Pianists also gauge intervals by muscular sensation, and as they can rehearse their movements away from

the piano, so a skilled organist can eventually rehearse his pedal movements away from the organ.

(5) All passages that include registration should be played from memory.

(6) All passages that contain an awkward 'turning' should be memorized. The turning can then be advanced, or postponed to a more convenient place.

(7) Fingering should never be altered more than is absolutely necessary.

(8) In the case of an unfamiliar organ, the stops should be memorized in the groups provided by the builder.

(9) Before performance, the player should decide where he may rest his feet.

The suggestions 5–9 will help any one who has to perform on an organ new to him: the aim in practice should be to form habits that need not be unduly disturbed by a change of surroundings.

4. *The Mind's Eye*

There are many who rely so much on sight that they believe they are unable to play by heart. But one can read a piece a hundred times without really learning it; and the best reader is not necessarily the most correct player in regard to detail. It comes to this—how much can be played from memory is a test of one's knowledge of a work. Therefore, the more one can think while studying, the less will one have to think during performance; the more one can see in music when practising, the less in the end need one look at it. Surely, saving of eye-strain is alone worth any extra trouble involved in memorizing music completely.

CHAPTER XIX

THE CONCERTO PLAYER

A CONCERTO is a collaboration, and to learn the solo part before the other is highly unsatisfactory. Instead, the soloist should study in a manner that will make the orchestral part seem at first even more important than his own. One may begin in different ways:

(1) If a pianist, the student finds another to be soloist, himself playing the orchestral part on a second piano.

(2) If not a pianist, he listens to the whole work on a gramophone, while looking at the written music.

(3) Should no record be available, he asks some one else to play on a piano the orchestral part, at the same time playing only small portions of his own, such as principal themes. This method can be used by every concerto player, and if, before any detail is added, the entire work is gone through more than once as suggested, the orchestral part will be remembered as a background for all future study.

1. *Soloist as Conductor*

It is essential to procure the orchestral score, and to mark on the soloist's edition names of instruments at all important entries; this is preferable to playing from the full score, which may burden visual memory with unnecessary detail. Every concerto player must know the entries as well as the conductor; otherwise he may be put out by an orchestral part he is not prepared to hear. Pianists, for example, having the first violins immediately behind them at a concert, will hear their part much more clearly than many others.

After going through the work completely a few times (playing only solo passages that can be correctly read at sight) the student should take it in small portions, but not yet without a pianist for orchestra. Study should now be very slow and more complete, though ornamental passages, including cadenzas, are best omitted.

Solitary practice should then take place, at which fingering is arranged for difficult portions; but when repeating any passage it is highly important to sing or 'think' orchestral parts interwoven with the soloist's.

Further slow rehearsals can follow (with pianist for orchestra), filling in every detail previously omitted; after which, the performer may practise his part by himself as much as he likes, provided he continues to connect the chief orchestral themes with his own.

2. *Cues*

It is necessary, of course, to know the orchestral interludes. The conductor is supposed to give the soloist his principal cues, but the latter should not require such help. If *tutti* are long, one can count bars as orchestral players do. For instance, in triple time, the bars can be counted thus: 123, 223, 323, 423, and so on. But after hearing them many times this should not be necessary, and it is better to think the *tutti* rather than practise them, which may form habits unwanted at a concert.

When a work is becoming familiar, it can be played along with an orchestral record; to do so helps one to adapt one's tempo to that of others. Headings, or starting-points, are necessary throughout; and when rehearsing with gramophone or pianist, the soloist should occasionally refrain from playing, so that he may practise rejoining the orchestra at different places.

Passages most likely to cause nervousness are those occurring after a *tutti*: feeling suddenly alone with all eyes upon him, the performer may come to grief unless he knows his part extremely well. On this account, extra preparation should be given to solo passages, especially to those following an orchestral climax. The novice must also be prepared to play in some passages without hearing himself; then he must rely on tactual and muscular sensation; otherwise, tone may be forced, and memory hampered by muscular strain.

3. *The Friendly Rehearsal*

The most celebrated players are usually allowed most time for rehearsal, and many a tiro has to be content with a 'run through'. But, just because every minute is precious, conductors will, as a rule, give the soloist some time beforehand; and to go through a work privately with the conductor is the greatest help of all. Many things, including tempo, can be discussed at leisure; and the wise performer will make minor alterations to suit the taste of the conductor, who will more readily help him in return: at a concert so much depends on give and take between the two.

The music should be taken to the orchestral rehearsal, but not consulted except for a required starting-place. If the concert is to take place later in the day, a soloist must save himself, playing calmly, in a detached frame of mind; by giving too much, he may be unable to give of his best at the concert. However often the conductor stops the orchestra, the soloist should remain undisturbed, saying to himself, 'This is not a concert; this is merely preparation'. And if he can treat a rehearsal in this mood, enjoying the pleasure of playing with an orchestra for its own sake, things are almost certain to go well.

It will be realized that the study of a concerto must be very thorough, but once the hard work is done it is easier to play from memory than a solo: the sonority alone gives a feeling of support. When thoroughly prepared, when encouraged by a friendly rehearsal, the soloist may forget to be nervous in public: the concerto player's mind is so occupied with all that is going on around him that there is little time for self-consciousness.

CHAPTER XX

THE SINGER

PIANISTS and organists may have to recall four or more parts simultaneously, while singers have but one. Why, then, should so many be afraid of forgetting? Those who develop voices when mature frequently lack the years of musical training every instrumentalist has to undergo as a matter of course—training that relegates musical habits to subconscious direction. Although possible to remember music without knowing anything about its theory, the safest memory is founded on musicianship; consequently, those who sing without a background of technical knowledge are greatly handicapped, and, having little to rely on but temperament, they have excuse for nervousness.

1. *Background*

The easiest part of most songs to remember is the melody; singers are usually afraid of forgetting either time or words. Now, in order to remember time one must know it, not only consciously, but subconsciously; and many never get beyond the stage of counting, inaccurately at that. Even when the musical line of a song has been mastered, enough attention is rarely given to the accompaniment; and the two must be interwoven in the mind by habit until they can be felt as one thing.

Many of the best singers of to-day have had pianistic training in youth; and to be able to play even portions of accompaniments is a great advantage: singers, like concerto players, can only feel safe when they memorize their part along with the instrumental one; through association and force of habit the latter will then suggest each vocal entry when its time is due. Like every instrumentalist, too, every singer should form a first impression of a work as a whole (its shape and mood), afterwards studying vocal part in relation to background, lastly the melody alone. An actor would not expect to interpret a character without knowing anything about it; yet there exist students strangely incurious about what they sing, as was one known to the writer, who, though performing at her lesson the well-known aria of Saint-Saëns, had to confess that she had never read the story of Delilah.

2. *Words*

The meaning of music should be for every performer both the first thought and the last. If an instrumentalist tries to think of notes, if a singer tries to think of words, it may be impossible to recall them; and this is why one may forget words one knows and understands perfectly well. To recall them, one must think not of them but of what they stand for. For example, if there occurs the word 'sky', a mental picture should be created of a sky, grey or blue, in harmony with the song; but if the mistake is made of giving attention to the word itself, memory may produce 'cloud' by mistake. Verbal habits, when interfered with, have a way of seizing on the closest association to mend a broken chain of thought, and this association may be far from relevant to the text. Sometimes no word is forthcoming, in which case the mental orchestra may cease functioning.

Language, like the feeling for time, must become subconscious; and to sing fluently in French, for example, it is necessary to reach the stage of thinking in French. It is not surprising that some singers forget, because, relying on a translation far from literal, they are content to reproduce words of which they know neither sense nor pronunciation. If, to a singer, the noun *été* and the verb *était* sound exactly alike, how is he to remember them? How, too, is he to make the meaning clear for others?

3. *Nervousness*

Although deep understanding of a song, together with good technique, removes many usual causes of nervousness, some singers are afraid of losing breath-control. Relaxation is the best antidote to this kind of fear; and to instructions in para. 1, p. 111, can be added the following suggestion. Standing in the position described, preparatory to performance, singers should relax the abdominal muscles, then those of the shoulders. To do this facilitates breathing and helps to release possible tension of the throat. While singing, those who are far-sighted should raise their eyes: they will feel less self-conscious than if meeting the eyes of listeners.

4. *The Accompanist*

For practice, a grand piano is preferable to an upright; otherwise, an accompanist's habits may be disturbed at a concert by the difference of tone quantity and also by the altered position of the music-desk.

Like vocalists, accompanists should study a new song as a whole, afterwards singing the vocal part when practising their own. Though accompaniments are rarely played from memory in public, the pianist should know a song so well that he can rectify a possible slip of the singer, act as prompter, if necessary—emergencies requiring a thorough knowledge of the music and freedom in the performance of it.

5. *Hints for the Singer*

Like other musicians, singers vary both in capacity and training; and how much of a song should be undertaken at first sight must be decided by the individual. But it is essential for all, however gifted, to refrain from performing a song too soon; every work should be learnt, not only emotionally, but intellectually.

(1) When using time-names, a habit should be formed of breathing according to the phrasing of the words.

(2) When learning the pitch of notes, it is a mistake to play them singly, imitating them one by one. The student who cannot play a phrase for himself should listen to it two or three times, then try to sing that phrase by imitation.

(3) Not until one is absolutely certain of the time should one attempt to sing a phrase as it is written. Time and pitch should be in their place before being embroidered with words.

(4) It is extremely helpful to sing the words on one note, not allowing breathing to disturb the time; this practice prepares the singer for an accompanist who will not 'give'.

(5) Silent practice should frequently take the place of audible singing. (See also para. 9, p. 38.)

LESSON I

'FAIREST ISLE', BY PURCELL

(1) Read the words without trying to learn them.

(2) Notice the shape of the song—two-part (bars 1–16 and 17–32).[1]

[1] Numbers within paragraphs refer to the bars of the pieces given as Lessons.

(3) If you are a pianist, play the accompaniment's bass with your left hand, the melody with your right. Note modulations.

(4) Clap the time values of melody notes from 1 to 8 (repeated 9–16). Compare with phrases at 17 and 25. Notice the difference in accompaniment.

(5) Play the entire accompaniment (or listen to it). Notice imitations in 4, 12, 17, 19, etc.

(6) Sol-fa will help you at this stage. Compare breathing-places in 6 and 14.

(7) Playing at least part of the accompaniment, sing the words of both verses once through. Arrange musical scheme, including climaxes. The first verse is peaceful; the second suggests a crescendo of feeling up to 16.

(8) With or without the piano, sing the vowel sounds only of the words. Concentrate on singing legato and strictly in time.

(9) Examine the words, making up your mind about shades of tone to suit the sense. It may help you to associate meaning with pitch. At 19, the rising fourth coincides with 'gladness'. The 'wand'rer' can be associated with the coming minor key. Compare words and mood with those of second verse.

(10) Repeat para. 3.

Second Rehearsal

(11) Repeat previous instructions, but at para. 7 begin with second verse. After para. 8, practise the whole song, doubling the strength of the consonants. Read Hint no. 5, p. 94.

Third Rehearsal

(12) Begin with the most difficult portions, analysing intervals if necessary.

(13) As this song is simple, you may now begin to sing from memory. Take each phrase and practise thus:

    i. Clap the time of the notes from memory.
    ii. Add the pitch, singing to 'la'.
    iii. Add the words; then revise from 1–8.

(14) Learn phrases 9–16 in the same way, and revise. Then sing 1–16, using words of both verses. Learn 17–32 as suggested above. If you forget the tune, make a conscious association. (At 12 and 13, one phrase ends and another begins on the same note.)

(15) *Final Test.* With closed eyes listen to the accompaniment. Sing audibly merely a few phrases here and there, imagining the others. If you are uncertain of any part, relearn it by sol-fa or interval. (See also Rules, p. 51.)

(16) *Sequence of Thought.* Those who have poor verbal memory should make out a résumé of the verse, thus: (1) name of the song, followed by description—(9) inhabitant of the 'Isle'—(10) concerning the inhabitant—(17) 'blessed' and 'gladness' follow 'peace'—(21) as a contrast follows the 'wand'rer'—(25) 'churl' can be linked up by alliteration with 'complaineth', and so on.

If you cannot remember a word, its initial can be helpful. 'Flag' and 'glorious' are in alphabetical order. But the best and safest way to learn words is through contiguity and through their connexion with the trend of the song. For example, 'brave and true' suggests the mood of the following verse. Senseless mnemonics should be avoided.

17. THE SINGER ASKS QUESTIONS

1. *Should I rehearse the words without the melody?*

Not unless associated with time. See Hint no. 4, p. 94; also para. 4, p. 44.

2. *Will it help me to write out the words?*

It will confuse visual memory unless you write them on pages, keeping them in their original position.

3. *When I find a portion very difficult to retain, verbally or musically, what should I do?*

Like an operatic singer, act that portion while you practise: gesture and feeling will help you to remember both music and words. It is helpful also to visualize a scene relevant to the song, and mentally associate the music with a place or happening in the imaginary scene.

4. *May I study the vocal part alone when I know the song as a whole?*
As much as you like.

5. *Will it help me to develop absolute pitch?*
Yes, it is almost necessary in some modern songs; and it is a great
advantage to those who sing in opera. (See Chapter XXIII, p. 112.)

LESSON II

'WIE BIST DU, MEINE KÖNIGIN?' BY BRAHMS, OP. 32, No. 9

This is a song in ternary form, the second part of which (bar 44)
begins in the tonic minor.

(1) After reading the words, listen to the introduction (1–5). You
will find these bars as interludes at 20, 39, and 60.

(2) Compare accompaniment with melody in 6–11 (modulation to
dominant), 25–30, and 65–70. Sometimes the parts move in unison.

(3) Clap the time values of the melody in the above portions. Note
differences at 30 and 70.

(4) 12–16 and 31–35 are alike. Compare with 71–76. At 69 the word
'Tod' is prepared for by F flat in the bass. This word can be the signal
for the singer's coming E double flat.

(5) 17–20. At 17, voice imitates accompaniment, but not exactly.
36–39 is the same passage. At 75 there is no bar of rest for the voice,
as previously; and from 75 to 79 the vocal part differs from the first
settings of the word 'wonnevoll'. Compare with 56–60.

(6) Compare 44–46 with 6–8. In 47 compare time of entry with 9.
There is a suggestion of D major; then a perfect cadence in A at 49.

(7) 50–55. Play bass of accompaniment with vocal melody more than
once. This passage has to be learnt as new material, though really the
first theme in disguise.

Throughout, the accompaniment sometimes follows the voice in
unison, sometimes not. The piece can be studied by playing each
separate part of the accompaniment in turn along with the vocal part
until the ear can tell the voice what to do. (See para. 3, p. 35.) It will
be understood why any irregularity of time can spoil this song: as in
many modern works, the instrumental and vocal parts are completely
'wrapt up' in one another.

H

Note. The instructions given in both Lessons should be adapted to suit the singer's quality of memory and also the type of song studied. If the singer has a method of his own that is dependable, he should not discard it. It is advisable, however, to read carefully the whole of this book, because all musicians' problems are much alike.

CHAPTER XXI

THE STRING PLAYER AND OTHERS

THE problems of instrumentalists who perform against a musical background resemble those of the singer. Chapter XX should be read with care; also Chapter XIX: in these are underlined the main ideas of this book which are especially applicable to music for the string and wind player.

After the preliminary study of the piece, the solo part may be taken alone and in detail, and, as suggested throughout the book, difficulties should be considered one by one. Bowing for the string player, breathing for the wind player, these should be consciously arranged to begin with, and, like fingering, considered in relation to phrasing.

1. *Nervousness*

Like singers, many instrumentalists have the responsibility, not only of remembering musical notes, but also that of forming them; and it is the fear of playing out of tune that troubles so many. But fear usually brings about what is feared; anxiety tightens the muscles, including those of the throat, and to such an extent that, though a musician can mentally hear a required note, he may be physically incapable of producing it. The writer met a man who had the experience of getting up to speak in public, only to find that through his anxiety to speak well he could not speak at all—no words were forthcoming. He sat down for a moment, and relaxed; immediately the habits of speech were able to perform as fluently as usual.

How is one to be sure of being able to relax at will? There is one way only—by forming a habit of it during practice. After study of the musical content of a passage, after due consideration of technical ways and means, one should try to find the right muscular condition, and then remember the sensations of playing freely; when these become habitual, the performer may safely relax his mind and leave the elaborate mechanism to subconscious direction. It is not always realized, however, that though one may feel relaxed, relaxation in performance can never be complete. The right condition is termed 'tonus'; which means that muscles unused, though not tensed, are yet ready for action—a physical state that coincides with the right mental state, 'attention minus effort'.

When it is realized what the inner mind is capable of, every musician will become more careful in practice, in performance more care-free.

CHAPTER XXII

THE CONDUCTOR

AN orchestral score is a musical chart so crowded that infinite labour may be required for the learning of it. This is especially true of some modern works, so complicated that, before hearing them played by orchestra, composers themselves may be unable to realize the complete effect of what they have written. On account of the time necessary for learning a score it is impossible for most conductors to direct from memory every work studied; yet if a musician can mentally hear a work in its entirety, while directing it in imagination, he does not require written music at a concert. But the conductor's responsibility is great; consequently, many hesitate to lay aside a score they know by heart from cover to cover.

Is it advisable to conduct from memory? Opinion is divided. Yet the fashion (if fashion it be) is growing, many finding a great advantage in having their eyes and left hand always free for musical direction.

1. *First Sight*

It has been said that there are two types of conductors—one who keeps his head in the score; another who keeps the score in his head. But to learn any score completely every one must bury himself in it to begin with, though people vary much in the amount they can hear at first sight: conducting calls for more than musicianship and temperament; and the greatest conductor is not necessarily the quickest reader. Either pianist or gramophone can be helpful when beginning a work, especially if complicated, or when little time is available; but score-reading improves with practice, and it must be realized that to depend on outside help is not the best way to develop inward hearing. The essential is, of course, to obtain an idea of a work first as a whole (either by reading or by hearing it played)—to sketch the outline, as a painter blocks out his picture. Themes should then be studied and carefully phrased; and comparison of their various appearances will help to keep in view the form of a piece as a whole.

Strings should be studied in a group, woodwind likewise; and gradually the musical design can be completed by other parts. There is so much to think of in a score that conductors probably suffer less from mind-wandering than instrumentalists at work; but for all study there should be a scheme, and for every repetition a reason.

Through study, a piece begins to take shape. Each instrument has its colour, each phrase its mood; and individual parts take life, like characters in a drama; it is for the conductor to control tempo, to imbue the music with his emotion; and eventually he makes it so much a part of himself that it becomes an edition of his own, and one bearing the mark of his character. But no musician dare allow the feelings to take entire control; and though gesture should be unconscious expression of music, much conscious association can and should be used in preparing any musical work.

2. *The Mental Score*

Because conductors are forced to study music so much and with such complete attention (a score is necessary at rehearsal) they have an unusually keen visual memory. On this account it is helpful to mark important entries on the score by an arrow. (An actor marks his entries in a play.) And, to make these arrows more attractive visually, they might be drawn in different colours according to the 'voices' they represent. For example, entries for strings might be coloured thus: first violins, violet; seconds, blue; violas, green; 'cellos, yellow; double-basses, red. Each group of instruments might have its entries marked in the same way—the highest of each group having a violet arrow as signal for entry; the seconds blue, and so on, according to the number of parts. Position on the page is enough to indicate the type of instrument about to play; an arrow's colour would indicate an entry of a particular part in that group. Later, when mental rehearsal takes place, the colours will be recalled subconsciously, and will prompt the conductor's gestures in public, while mentally he turns the pages. But in marking scores discretion is necessary: musicians who give too much attention to marking music are not necessarily learning it rightly; and, as Sir Adrian Boult once said to the author, 'Those who over-mark their scores may end by remembering marks instead of music.'

It is advisable always to use the same edition of music; otherwise, if a student studies a miniature score to begin with, and then puts before him another upon which entries and everything else are differently placed, visual memory is bound to be confused. Indeed, a change of edition is quite enough to bring complete disaster to any musician's private orchestra of habits.

It was stated on p. 44 that to write out a passage would not help an instrumentalist to recall it more easily from memory; but the conductor's case is different. Not having to play the notes subconsciously, he would find it helpful to write out from memory a few bars of any part particularly difficult to retain.

3. *Associations*

An orchestral plan should be made on paper; with this on a table at home the student can rehearse a work, pointing to different groups of players when their entry is due. This form of study should be followed by silent rehearsal without the chart, now making necessary signals to different parts of the room, where, in imagination, he sees the players. Though the best conductors do not consciously arrange their gestures, it is helpful, while hearing music mentally, to associate sound and mood by occasionally sketching in miniature the gestures of a complete performance.

One who prefers to use the score in public will find an advantage in being able to turn pages without thinking; and to form this habit music can be rehearsed from memory with a large book of blank pages, which are turned when the musician's visual memory tells him to.

4. *Repetition*

Much time and labour can be saved by well-spaced repetition. (See p. 51.) But because the middle of a long movement is usually the most elaborate portion, extra time and attention must be given to this; 'slow motion' rehearsal makes clear the beauty of detail. (See para. 6, p. 45.)

No one should pore over scores for too long at a time; a walk round the room is often advisable. Even better is the short rest period at definite intervals, occupied by a walk in the open air. (Conductors, like instrumentalists, sometimes find it helpful to rehearse their music mentally when walking.) See also para. 2, p. 34.

5. *Concertos*

When learning a concerto score, the conductor should give his first thought to the solo part; he will then understand the right tempo from the soloist's point of view. (Speed of a preliminary *tutti* should correspond.) Some piano passages, for example, are ineffective (perhaps impossible) if taken at a tempo that may appeal to conductors relieved of the responsibility of playing them with their fingers. In vocal work, tempo should be decided by the singer's convenience. Though technical, these points concern memory: nervousness is infectious, and a possible mistake of the soloist may upset the conductor just as much as a mistake of his own. Therefore, even when a concerto score is learnt by heart, it should always lie on his desk at a concert.

6. *Choral Work*

Those who have experienced the freedom of performing from memory may possibly wish their choir to do likewise. Extra work involved will be amply repaid, because whether or not a conductor gains from appearing 'without book', a choir most certainly does. To hear and see the turning of pages during some choral works can be very distracting for an audience; and when the singers' attention is divided between score and conductor, their work lacks an imaginative quality missed only by those who have heard a choir that sings by heart. An American choirmaster, who had trained his singers to perform from memory, said that at once they became 'a totally different choir'.

Many of the hints given in Chapter XX should prove helpful in choral work; the practice of singing words on one note, strictly in time, is specially recommended. (See para. 4, p. 94.)

7. *Nervousness*

Although the conductor's responsibility is greater than that of any soloist, he has so much to attend to during performance that he will have little time for thoughts of self. Besides, having his back to the hall, he will be less likely to suffer from self-consciousness than a soloist who has to face the public. But the soloist has only one instrument to play upon; the conductor a hundred—the minds of his players; and unless he understands human nature as thoroughly as the music he directs, his task will be doubly hard. Here it is impossible to do more than touch on the effect of a conductor's character on his own nerves and those of his men; but without goodwill on both sides, rehearsal can be fruitless: after three hours of strain and mutual misunderstanding, it is unlikely that either orchestra or conductor will be free from nervousness at the subsequent performance, or in the mood to give of their best. An ambitious student should himself play in an orchestra if he wishes to understand the players' point of view. He will then appreciate the unconscious irritation caused by continual stopping for correction better postponed, and also the mental strain all orchestral players have to undergo, even when treated with consideration.

A conductor must take no risks: he should always use the score if, for any reason, he doubts his memory; and to have it there, closed, will give confidence to others who know their music, but who, nevertheless, feel a responsibility both towards their players and their art. Though impressed by conducting from memory, the public does not demand the banishment of scores; and as conductors have their back to the hall, listeners are not so distracted by the turning of pages as in the case of soloists. It is for the individual to decide whether or not he should conduct from memory.

V

CHAPTER XXIII

CONCERNING MEMORY

1. New Practice for Old

ANY student with experience of teaching knows that, even if tired, it is possible to concentrate on music lessons for hours on end. Many teachers confess that they know their pupils' pieces better than their own, which is not surprising, considering they have given them complete attention. Even the most scatter-brained pupil can concentrate fully during a whole hour of an interesting lesson; and, as it is stimulating to work in company, the writer believes that much music might profitably be learnt in this way. If the university student can gain by sharing his problems with another, why not the student of music? A practitioner who suffers from mind-wandering when alone would especially benefit by collaboration.

With one piano, much might be done; with two pianos, even more; and the division of parts previously suggested (now between the hands of both players), would clarify the first impression of music apparently complicated. The learning of a fugue, for example, would become comparatively simple if each player had but one or two parts to attend to, instead of three or four. (See para. 3, p. 35.) Would not many interesting things in music come to light through discussion? Could not time be saved by a competition in the speed of learning? People often complain that they cannot afford to take lessons, but co-operative practice would cost nothing except extra thought. Many students do not wish to take the trouble of thinking; they practise inadequately, relying on a teacher to tell them what to do; in consequence, every advanced teacher has to waste time in pointing out things that pupils of average intelligence are quite capable of finding out for themselves. Co-operative practice would teach students to become more self-reliant; and periods of solitary work between 'meetings' could be arranged for development of the ideas discussed. Co-workers should preferably be about the same stage of musical development; otherwise, one or other may take up the attitude of a dogmatic teacher, defeating the end of joint practice, which should be self-development and the development of concentration through added interest in study.

Though no one should be discouraged by unjust criticism, every one should be willing to consider the effect of his work on others. A painter will hold a looking-glass in front of his picture in order to see it differently; and another point of view can be enlightening. Mutual criticism could prevent the appearance of many bad habits: one can be oblivious to one's own. So much can be learnt merely by hearing oneself play to others; and without a teacher, students might form a class for the practice of performance—experience invaluable to the future concert artist, who cannot always work alone, because music, for its fullest enjoyment, has to be shared.

The Dumb Piano

The dumb piano is less in use than formerly, which is to be regretted, because a student who mentally hears the sound of the silent notes can greatly benefit from 'dumb' practice. (A practice clavier was used by Liszt.) Apart from anything else, a pianist who knows that others cannot be disturbed will practise with more concentration—an advantage in the modern apartment.

Many teachers believe that a dumb keyboard encourages mechanical playing, but a piano does not necessarily bring about musical practice; and silent keyboards (like others) can be useful or useless according to whether the student listens or not. If used by a beginner for ear-training, instead of (as formerly) for training of muscles only, dumb practice can help to co-ordinate aural and muscular habits. The small keyboard can be used only for preliminary ear-training and technical exercises; but longer keyboards are made, including one (folding up for convenience in travelling) upon which complete pieces can be memorized and rehearsed. A full keyboard (mounted on legs) is the best for home practice, though incomplete without the addition of pedals. The action of a dumb keyboard is never the same as that of a piano with dampers of varying size and weight, but the two are sufficiently alike to make silent practice profitable in many ways, especially to the pianist on tour. Apart from anything else, exercise improves circulation; and warm hands mean better technique.

2. TECHNIQUE AND FINGERING

Memory is frequently blamed for a break-down for which technique is primarily responsible; and because any passage involving a struggle may interfere with memory, no performer should risk playing in public music beyond his powers of execution.

Those who complain of unreliable memory are usually tense; and if persuaded to relax their muscles, their memory immediately improves. But if a performer doubts his memory, muscles may become so cramped that the habits will not be able to function at all. Due attention, therefore, should be given to the necessary elasticity of technique. In rapid passages, no pianist's arm should rest heavily on the keyboard: arm relaxation, necessary in slow singing passages, in quick passages may so hamper a player's movements that he may be unable to continue. For the sake of memory alone, a difficult passage containing a long crescendo should not be begun too loudly: the functioning of memory depends greatly on knowing how to save oneself physically, not only before, but during performance.

As technical freedom assists memory, so does playing from memory assist technique. There are players with eyes fixed upon the music who have never experienced mental freedom; but when these learn to trust subconscious memory, technique becomes much more fluent, and without additional exercise.

Fingering

Those who have 'absolute pitch' are less liable to be upset by a change of fingering than others who depend greatly on muscular memory. But because a badly fingered passage may be difficult to play, it is advisable for every one to finger all passages consistently, and with reference to their final tempo.

(1) A required legato should not be broken unless unavoidable.

(2) If possible, short notes should be fingered so as to avoid a break between them and the accents they prefix. (See para. 7, pp. 27–8, also Ex. *c*, p. 26.)

(3) Sequences and patterns of notes (or chords) can frequently be fingered alike. Repetitions help muscular memory.

Ex. *a*. Debussy, Prelude, Vol. 1, No. 8.

Ex. *b*. Scriabin, Op. 16, No. 3.

The mistake many make is in learning notes and fingerings without reference to interpretation and tempo; but when the phrasing of music is defined at the outset, fingering becomes simple, because logical. (See also para. 2, pp. 34–5.)

3. HEALTH

To musicians health is as important as work. But teachers, especially, seem to forget the necessity of sufficient exercise and regular meals: to sit in a chair all day, to 'snatch' food at odd minutes, cannot be good for any one; and after years of such habits, health deteriorates and with it memory. If only for the sake of pupils, a teacher should try to keep well: one who is 'nervy' can be trying for a pupil of any age.

The touring artist has an even more exacting life than the teacher. Subject to constant change of surroundings and altitude, all habits, including those of sleep, must be highly adaptable.

1. *Diet*

Diet is important, but especially so during the weeks before a concert; if the performer eats too little of the right foods, he will feel depressed and probably unusually apprehensive. Food, like work, is best digested at regular hours. But, like the actor, the musician should never eat immediately before playing in public; it is essential, however, to have one good meal on a concert day, preferably several hours before the event. Because musical performance requires energy, sugar is recommended by doctors as a tonic for the musician. Easily digested, it forms a valuable food before and during a concert day.

Strong stimulants should be barred; likewise drugs of all sorts; for the musician who knows how to relax, these are unnecessary, and to make oneself dependent on any drug is to form a habit psychologically harmful. A cup of weak tea with light refreshment may be taken a couple of hours before a concert; but even tea should be avoided if too stimulating. As one can make oneself nervous merely by drinking too much coffee, it will be realized that diet may have not a little to do with the behaviour of memory.

2. *Exercise*

Cold affects the responsiveness of the nerves, and however retentive memory may be, the habits of recall are hampered by a bad circulation. Besides, the musician with a good circulation requires comparatively little work in order to keep in practice. No musician should begin the day without doing physical exercises (which should never take the form of 'jerks'); and any daily exercises of the right kind are much more beneficial than occasional and long walks at a time when much energy is required for musical work. Like singers, instrumentalists should also practise breathing exercises, some of which may be done rhythmically while walking. Besides teaching self-control, such exercises bring a glow of physical well-being, which inevitably increases self-confidence.

4. RELAXATION

There is no doubt that music is good for health; but practice wears both nerves and muscles, and time must be allowed for necessary repairs to take place; if not, memory suffers: many a break-down is due to nothing but fatigue. Every practitioner should relax for a few minutes both before work and before a meal. A short rest should also be taken later in the day, if only for ten minutes.

Trying to relax at any time will prevent relaxation, because it can only be attained through withdrawal of effort. Here we can learn something from animals, which know how to rest even when awake. (Lift the paw of your dog while it is resting, and you will notice how loose all the joints are, and how heavily the limb lies in your hand.) So much energy is wasted, on the contrary, by civilized human beings; there are few who are truly reposeful; hands and feet are restless when there is no call for action. The student who can learn to inhibit unnecessary movement will begin to attain what is known as 'poise'; and to be able to relax muscles at will helps both to conserve energy and to prevent nervousness. At any time when nervous or irritable, one has but to relax; then mental tension is relieved.

1. Restful Posture

Musicians should form a habit of sitting thus: hands lie limply on the lap; feet (not crossed) are placed one in advance of the other (soles on the ground). The position of hands should reverse that of feet—when right foot is farther forward than left, the left hand should lie on the lap in advance of the right; and vice versa. The hands should not touch. This position may be assumed when travelling, or at any quiet moment; and immediately before performance it helps to bring about a sense of mental and physical repose, when shoulders and arms are really relaxed.

Singers on the platform should stand with their weight divided between the feet, one of which should be farther forward than the other. Hands should be held together; and, as in the sitting posture described previously, they should reverse the position of the feet. For example, when the left foot is foremost, the right hand should cover the left hand, and vice versa. One can stand in this position for a long time without fatigue.[1]

Pianists should sit up, with arched back: by moving from the hips (without relaxing at the waist, as many do) much fatigue can be avoided. When damper pedal is being used, the left foot can be placed under the chair: this helps to balance the body.

2. Restful Work

Some people seem to dread any form of rest when awake, apparently believing they can do nothing useful unless their feet are on the ground. But with feet up there is less fatigue, and tall people will especially benefit by doing some of their work in this position, including mental rehearsal of complete pieces. A good moment for this restful practice is last thing at night; the subconscious mind will then continue to work without conscious assistance. This suggestion, however, is only for those who sleep well.

[1] For these relaxation postures the writer is indebted to her friend, Miss G. Reith.

3. *Sleep*

It is not the over-strained who sleep best, but those who know how to conserve energy; and to be able to sleep at will is one of the secrets of good memory. Insomnia, like nervousness, will disappear most quickly if not talked about; but some people seem proud of insomnia, and by the daily suggestion, 'I am a very bad sleeper', they confirm a bad habit. To sleep is a natural habit; and unless there is a definite physical cause for insomnia, every healthy person ought to be able to sleep at regular hours. Conscious life, like a serial story, should be discontinued every night at the same time. But in order to enjoy eight hours of freedom from worry, one must learn to turn one's back on unnecessary worries during the day: to be light-hearted when awake is the best preparation for restful sleep.

After performing at a concert, a musician may feel unable to sleep; in that case, after having something to eat, he should take a walk. (A soporific game like 'patience' can help to relax the mind.) But even if not sleeping, one can rest; and to rest, as an animal does, by relaxing completely, is most enjoyable; those who can, will no longer dread lying awake occasionally. Worry is the usual cause of insomnia, and it is worry about insomnia that makes it habitual.[1]

4. *Silence*

Although it requires practice to learn to sleep well after performing at a concert, every musician ought to be able to sleep beforehand. But the modern ear is bombarded by sound waves, and as few well-trained musicians can hear without listening, special precautions should be taken against disturbance before a concert. Ear-plugs of cotton-wool are useless, but soaked in glycerine they become most effectual. Better still are those of fine wax that are obtainable; and provided with these the most sensitive musician can become oblivious to everything but dreams.

5. ABSOLUTE PITCH

The sense of relative pitch is a necessity for artistic performance; but absolute pitch is another matter, and for some instrumentalists not

---

[1] In the author's *Musical Secrets* will be found another paragraph on relaxation and sleep.

essential. Yet, though it may sometimes prove confusing (as when music is played in a different key from that in which it is written), on the whole it is a great advantage, especially where memory is concerned: upon hearing a sound mentally or physically, one who has 'pitch' can instinctively play that note. It does not follow, however, that this type of player is necessarily musical in other ways.

Is it possible to develop this faculty, called by T. H. Pear 'absolute tone-memory'? Memory for everything varies in the individual: some learn French quickly; others slowly; others never learn to think in French however long they study. But though training cannot supply something mentally lacking in the individual, it is surprising what training can do. Those who believe they have no memory for music can eventually learn to play by heart with great fluency; and it is possible for many (if not all) musical people to develop memory for pitch, and by the same means—patient and regular practice. The existence of human 'lightning calculators' does not discourage the study of arithmetic; yet those who have no natural memory for pitch rarely make any effort to acquire it. This form of memory is, of course, dependent on association. Some instrumentalists associate pitch with locality on a keyboard; other musicians, including many singers, associate pitch with muscular sensation of placing a note. Repetition always deepens associations, and many string players remember the sound of open strings, just because these have to be tuned so often and with complete attention.

Below is a new method for acquiring absolute pitch through association. Memory tests should be very short and frequent; practitioners should listen with closed eyes in order to centre attention on the quality of sound.

1. *Preliminary Test*

After relaxing mentally and physically, the student should imagine the beginning of any piece he knows by heart, and if he can mentally hear it in its original key, he partially possesses absolute pitch, though he may require a good deal of practice in order to recognize by ear the key of music unfamiliar.

Tactual and aural memory are sometimes so closely associated that it may be enough merely to touch the surface of a key in order to bring to consciousness the exact pitch of that note. An amateur gifted with absolute pitch, who was unable to obtain a piano, amused himself by improvising mentally, but this he was unable to do without a keyboard of cardboard upon which to play silently.

2. *Original Method for acquiring Absolute Pitch*

The student should concentrate on remembering the pitch of one sound at a time, along with its tonic chord. To represent a key, a familiar piece should be chosen, such as the National Anthem, which may be used for memorizing G major. After playing three phrases, the student should sing G, concentrating on the sound's colour—its quality. He should then sing the tonic chord in arpeggio two or three times, and later in the day try to recall the sound of G along with the effect of its chord, using a piano as prompter. An attempt to recall should not be too conscious; rather, one should expectantly wait for the sound to come to consciousness. Some days may pass (possibly weeks) before the sound can be recalled at will; but when this happens, the beginning of another familiar piece should be chosen to represent another key-note, preferably one like D flat, because not easily confused with G. (The latter should also be kept up by rehearsal.)

It is, of course, possible to remember one sound in connexion with another by relative pitch. The quickest reader, however, does not have to think (even subconsciously) about intervals: he associates a written sign with its place on the keyboard; and the aim of the method given here is to develop aural memory for individual notes. If this can be done, muscular response is immediate.

Note by note should be added in the same way, associating a chosen piece with a particular key; and in time the whole chromatic scale can be completed. A tuning-fork is useful for memory tests at odd minutes. On certain days the learner may find memory much more accurate than on others; but if patient, he will probably receive a pleasant surprise. One day, when listening to the radio, he will say to himself with conviction, 'That piece is in the key of D.' He will recognize the key without thinking, because subconscious memory has been trained through association.

3. *Natural Memory*

Absolute pitch usually brings with it natural memory for music heard or played; yet for those who have this spontaneous memory there is a possible danger, because, if a player relying entirely on ear forgets (through nervousness, perhaps) the sound of music he plays, he will be unable to continue as another would who had learnt it more consciously. Even if failure of aural memory should interrupt performance, consciousness, like a prompter, ought to be able to start the playing again through knowledge of smaller parts of the work in relation to the whole. Those, therefore, who can immediately reproduce music heard or played, are advised to analyse their concert pieces just as carefully as others differently gifted. (See also para. 16, p. 54.)

6. Improvisation

A musician gifted with absolute tone memory is usually able to improvise naturally. Yet the power to improvise, like that of recognizing the pitch of sounds, can be acquired to a greater or lesser extent through development of memory: the student who learns harmony by playing chords in musical sequence will consciously form a repertoire of chords which he will eventually be able to combine subconsciously. In the case of both pitch and improvisation, however, the natural gift usually far surpasses the power acquired.

Although consciousness may decide sequence of key and shape, true improvisation is subconscious; and on this account it is difficult for many to crystallize their best improvisation in the form of written composition. Conscious thought may interrupt the flow of ideas.

A supreme improviser, an amateur with no conscious knowledge of harmony, who can produce any kind of music at will (including elaborate counterpoint), confesses he is conscious of 'pre-hearing' only one note (or chord) in advance of his hands.

Composers sometimes find it difficult to play their own works from memory; but this is not surprising, because when a piece is finished they frequently lose interest in it. And as a piece is rarely completed without alteration of the first draft, this alone is enough to account for any difficulty experienced by a composer in recalling the final edition.

One whose playing is laboured is unlikely to improvise well; but **if** any performer is playing a piece freely, subconsciousness may give **him** a surprise: the familiar piece sounds quite new; like an improvisation it seems to well up from the inner mind; and when this beautiful experience is his, the musician may know that he is playing, in every sense of the word, by heart.

7. MEMORY FOR OTHER THINGS

1. *Names*

Some people remember names much more easily than others; but memory can be developed, as in the case of music—by means of attention, association, and repetition.

To say 'I have a shocking memory for names' will not improve matters; instead, one should try to get interested, not only in names, but in those they represent. Any arresting name (like an unusual chord) is easily retained, as is one that causes amusement; and if, for example, a very big person is called Little, it is unlikely that name will be forgotten. A common name (like a common chord) is more difficult to recall; and it should be consciously associated with something else connected with the person it belongs to. (See para. 16, p. 96.) Of course, if a person is met very often, repetition alone will strengthen the memory for a name, but should you forget it, do not try to remember. Instead, think round the name, visualizing the place where you met its owner, recalling everything you can connected with him. If associations prove unsuccessful, turn attention to other things; and at an unexpected moment the name will probably return to consciousness. It should then be written down, because writing involves both muscular and visual memory.

2. *Faces*

Few resent the forgetting of their name by a stranger, but many strongly resent being personally forgotten; and though one need not hesitate to ask a person to repeat his name, one should never make the admission, 'I do not remember your face.' We should follow the example of Leonardo da Vinci, who, though profoundly interested in physiognomy, thought it advisable to evolve an elaborate method to assist visual memory. Any method of our own should be based on association; it is helpful, for example, to associate the face of a stranger with that of a previous acquaintance. Above all, one should try to penetrate the face, which is usually a mask; and if interested in the real person one is speaking to (instead of thinking of one's own reactions concerning him), one is much more likely to remember his face.

As it is a great advantage to a public performer to remember names and faces of passing acquaintances, a note-book should be kept in which to jot down daily the names of strangers met, along with any details about them. Recent additions to the portrait gallery should be revised frequently, and faces called up mentally as clearly as possible. If this is done regularly, it will be found that the faculty for remembering both names and faces will greatly improve: knowing that one is going to note them afterwards, one will, on first acquaintance, give both more attention.

Even far-sighted people can go round the world, see everything, yet notice little. Noticing can become a habit. When travelling, for instance, there is plenty of opportunity for development of visual memory: with the eye of a detective one can practise 'registering' people; one can look them up and down, then try to recall from memory their features, clothes, what they may be carrying—an entertaining exercise, this, requiring active attention.

In recording anything, the essential is to see it clearly as a whole and in smaller portions also. (The great staff of eleven lines is divided up to make its contents clear to the eye.) Even the learning of a telephone number can be simplified by dividing numerals into groups, which can be memorized, like musical phrases, by comparison one with another.

People who do not visualize music may yet visualize other things very clearly; and on this account it is advisable to take notes of things to be seen to, including appointments. Those who do so with complete attention, and who see the words in their own writing, will not readily forget them.

3. *Intentional Forgetting*

When we forget a thing, we mean we are unable to recall it; and concerning the amount that can be recalled at any period of life, the mind apparently exerts economy: what we do not require we tend to forget. Certain things are shoved into the background to make way for others temporarily more useful; and after putting music aside for some time, one may be able to play from memory comparatively few pieces of a previously large repertoire; but after a few days the habits get into practice, and the apparently forgotten pieces return to consciousness. Therefore, the amount remembered consciously concerning any one subject is limited, to a great extent, by temporary requirement. But should much be needed, the mind will respond: when memory is rightly used, its subconscious capacity is seemingly unlimited.

One may find, however, that one consistently forgets certain facts and not others, certain appointments, certain pieces of music; and for this there is usually a very good reason. Let us open our book of experience, where are pictures both pleasant and unpleasant; but in the less recent chapters we shall probably find the pleasant predominating. Why should this be? Memory is not as freakish as it appears: what the mind finds disagreeable or unbearably painful, it will endeavour to forget. In order to deal with apparent vagaries of memory, it is necessary to recognize this capacity of the mind to erase associations unpleasant or painful. It is easy to remember anything connected with some one we like very much; but if our feeling becomes dislike, or if we do that person a wrong, memory concerning this individual will be affected: we may find one day that we have completely forgotten his address, though previously it was as familiar as our own.

'Intentional forgetting' provides yet another reason for making the practice of music pleasurable: mechanical work, over-work, cramming, all bring in their train such a distaste for music studied that the mind may revolt. There is then a strike of memories, which will completely paralyse the habits of recall.

4. *Dreams and Memory*

Those who know how to relax will best remember their dreams. On waking, to go over all one can recall of them is an excellent exercise. After some practice it is surprising how much will come to the surface; and to get in touch with one's subconscious mind in this way will greatly improve memory for everything, including music.

VI

It is better to be a crystal and be broken,
Than to remain perfect like a tile upon the housetop.
From the Chinese.

CHAPTER XXIV

FROM FEAR TO CONFIDENCE

SOME good performers who confess they are nervous in public are not nervous in the usual sense; their state is rather one of excitement amounting to exaltation.

1. *Nervousness of Different Kinds*

Excitement may be called the right kind of nervousness, because, instead of being a deterrent, it brings about increased sensibility and increased endurance, enabling the interpreter to surpass himself. The mental temperature of an inspired performer cannot be said to be normal, and it might well be described as *Lampenfieber*,[1] because less often experienced by day than in the evening. But, on the contrary, *Lampenfieber* is synonymous with *le trac*—a state of mind in which fears develop so alarmingly that mental paralysis may result. There is a form of this nervousness for which the musician is responsible; others over which he has less apparent control; but though these may have physical causes, such as cold hands (or a bad piano) and physical effects (including cold hands), all nervousness is psychical. To prevent or to cure it, the student should bury himself in his book of experience, for there only is to be found either safeguard or remedy.

2. *A Dangerous Idea*

In the mind of most of us will be found a desire for sympathy, and the student who says with a shiver, 'I am so nervous', is like the child who enjoys being ill because it attracts attention. This kind of nervousness is a form of vanity, and just as people may say they suffer from insomnia, though sleeping tolerably well, some performers pretend to be more nervous than they are. One who discusses his fears, however,

---

[1] Translated literally, 'lamp fever'.

may find his last state worse than the first, because attention increases nervousness; even to think of it is dangerous, and to name it even more so. Like a jinnee, if given freedom, it can develop into a force with which a musician may feel powerless to cope. It is one thing to boast of nervousness in a circle of friends; quite another to be humiliated by a break-down in public: fear materialized through experience will gather round it so many unpleasant emotions that a complex will form—a mental entanglement that self-knowledge alone can unravel. It is unsafe to entertain the thought of fear in any form; and the only time safe to speak of it (even to oneself) is when, in a detached frame of mind, one is seeking the cause of it.

3. *Searching Questions*

On a first night an actor is excusably nervous; having to collaborate with others possibly more nervous, he may be given a wrong cue—an emergency upsetting even to the well prepared. But unless associated with an uncertain accompanist or conductor, the soloist ought to stand in a much stronger mental position than the actor; and a victim to the wrong kind of nervousness should ask himself questions such as these: 'Do I always learn music conscientiously? Do I leave any passage to luck? Do I do everything humanly possible to make performance a success?' Paderewski gives his experience. 'For many years in my career I had that terrible pain before playing—that anguish which is not to be described. My theory was that that terrible inside nervousness, fear of everything—of the public, of the piano, of the conditions, of the memory—that was nothing else but a bad conscience.' He adds: 'Fright is only the sense of insecurity, and it may be insecurity of only one passage or phrase . . . that passage can torment you as long as it remains unconquered.'[1]

4. *Untimely Practice*

Though frequently caused by inadequate work, the sense of insecurity may be caused by over-work; terrified to trust themselves, many performers rehearse their music again and again at the very time when they should not think of it. Conscious work should be finished long before

[1] *My Story.*

a concert; and if ten days beforehand (preferably ten weeks) a performer does not know his programme thoroughly, he will probably be nervous, possibly unsuccessful. Even if a piece has to be learnt at short notice, as is sometimes unavoidable, it is rarely advisable to do analytical work at the last moment. Those about to perform most successfully may feel as if their conscious mind were a blank, which is a sign that responsibility has been relegated to the subconscious: this, then, is not the moment for self-prompting. Experienced musicians know that to perform in public is usually more alarming in prospect than in reality; merely to touch the keyboard of their instrument revives mental associations which, if not hampered by doubt, will function through force of habit.

There are many who insist on practising up to the last moment, who, nevertheless, 'get through'; among these, performers both experienced and successful who feel they cannot face their public without a last-minute rehearsal; but if music is learnt rightly, surely this is unnecessary. Of course, if the mind is not anxious, there is less danger in last-minute practice; but at the end, it is always safer to practise too little rather than too much. Eleventh-hour workers, it should be noted, are frequently unusually nervous at a concert; and this is not surprising, because, apart from possibly worrying their minds, they have tapped their supply of nervous energy too soon. It is difficult to persuade the over-worker to rest before performance; yet to prove memory's retention, one has but to play a concert programme a week afterwards—in which interval it has been laid aside—and just because memory has not been disturbed, it will then recall the music with unusual ease. Only by means of such an experiment can an anxious musician learn either the value of faith in memory or the benefit of relaxation.

5. *Discouragement*

One of the commonest causes of nervousness is extraneous suggestion —an idea of failure received by the mind when off its guard, which may develop into a devastating autosuggestion. The writer has met numberless people crippled by fear apparently arising from the experience of a break-down in public; but behind it, the real cause of it, was parent, teacher, or examiner, who, by adverse suggestion, had developed in the student's mind a sense of inferiority in the place of faith. In some cases, discouragement had been given in small doses, slowly robbing the student of self-confidence; in others, given in one fatal dose, enough to kill all enterprise. A young person is seldom enough of a psychologist to realize the effect of adverse suggestion, or to comprehend its motives: the parent who withholds all encouragement may do so out of jealousy of youth; the teacher who thwarts a pupil's development may have sadistic tendencies, or be merely too tired to be human; the examiner who reduces a candidate to tears in public may himself suffer from a sense of inferiority. Helpful criticism is one thing; destructive criticism quite another; and both student and artist must learn to defend themselves against adverse suggestion given by others through selfish motives. Though the young are especially sensitive, older people, too, may be checkmated by suggestion of the wrong kind; even a stray remark of a sympathetic friend may bring disaster if failure is suggested (however innocently) to any one unprepared to ignore it.

6. *Mental Repair*

It is as useless, however, to resent discouragement as stupid to believe one is unique in experiencing it. Every student should read the lives of people who have done great things, if only to learn that adverse criticism and disappointment, enough to poison some minds, can be to others a tonic. The greater an artist, the less often does he satisfy the critic within himself. Like a student, every successful artist has moments of despondency; being human, he may forget a passage in public; he may possibly break down and be unable to finish a piece. (Even von Bülow was known to have a lapse of memory at a concert.) But instead of talking about such an experience, of thinking about it for the rest of his life, he does the only intelligent thing—he endeavours to play better next time.

Discouragement can take so many forms, yet all can be turned to good account, including the break-down, if regarded as a passing accident, instead of as a hopeless disaster. After apparent failure, a performer should pick himself up mentally; because, like a flyer who has crashed, he will lose his nerve if he does not try again. He should then examine his mental equipment with all honesty by means of these questions:

'Did I go on the platform expecting to break down? Was I tired that night? Was I thinking of myself instead of the music?' When the cause of an accident is discovered (there may be more causes than one), the event should be considered as a form of experience; if accepted mentally as a help for the future, fear surrounding it will begin to disperse; and instead of being crippled by an accident, the mind of a performer may become stronger than before, as a broken bone may be, when rightly set.

7. *Unexpected Encouragement*

Provided a performer puts his heart into his music, both public and critics will always forgive some wrong notes; they will even forgive a slight lapse of memory (if they notice it, which is not always the case); and to bear this in mind helps to prevent the fear of these faults—the fear that usually causes them.

On the platform, any fault should be ignored by the performer; otherwise, discouraged by a slip, he may ruin a whole programme. Some parts may be good; others less good, but one must learn to listen to oneself serenely and to hope for the best. There is an aspect of public performance to be faced unselfishly: musical effects too consciously made sound laboured; and when most satisfied with what one does, one may not satisfy an audience; though every note is in its place, every prearranged effect realized, the public may be left cold. On another occasion, when technique is imperfect, when memory plays tricks through nervousness, the music may convey more meaning. Now the public is sometimes the better critic; and when applause is heartfelt, a discouraged musician may be partially comforted for falling short of what he considers highest achievement.

8. *Overcoming Nervousness*

The mistake many make is in 'fighting' nervousness; but to try to suppress fear merely makes it worse, and those who understand the law of reversed effort will prefer the law of Tolstoi—'non-resistance'. Instead of lingering over an unpleasant memory of failure, the wise musician will at once turn his thoughts to a previous occasion when he was particularly successful; pleasant emotion will then replace fear, which gradually fades away if given no attention. Only when considered as a useful lesson can past failure be turned to good account; brooding over unpleasant memories makes them difficult to dispel—repetition strengthens all associations—and by consciously taking a cheerful line of thought one can bring about a mood of confidence.

But even by day the subconscious mind can behave most unreasonably, and sometimes a nervous musician seems incapable of helping himself; he feels powerless to think of anything but past and future failure. His first impulse may be to seek sympathy, but this should be his last resort. Instead, he should seek refuge in distraction—museum, theatre, cinema, or enthralling work apart from music—anything that will completely occupy attention for the time being. (A game of bridge may do.) Fear may return, but the sufferer will now be better able to cope with it, because experience has proved that fear can be replaced by interest sufficiently intense. Since any form of nervousness is accentuated by fatigue, the simple expedient of inviting a cheerful friend to a good dinner may banish the mood entirely.

In all cases of obsession the essential is to release mental tension, if only for a short period; after which, the victim will feel less helpless. In extreme cases the right psychiatrist can be consulted, but any one who can cure himself, instead of relying on another, will be safer in the end.

9. *Creating a Mood*

Thought of failure is always ready to attack the unwary or the weak, and the musician's mind must be protected by a mask of confidence, at first assumed, which becomes in time a part of his character. Though mood is subconscious, consciousness, by acting a state of mind, can help to bring it about. There is, therefore, what might be termed the 'law of reversed mood': when nervous, it is a great help merely to pretend to be calm.

To his closest friend a nervous player should never allow that he dreads the prospect of public appearance; he should never allow it even to himself. To friends or to himself he should say with a smile of confidence, 'I look forward to my concert', and if he says this often enough, audibly or silently, he will feel less and less afraid. This autosuggestion should be associated with a picture of success, regarded not as an unlikely dream, but as a certain and rightful reward for work well done. Some people think more in pictures than others, but in all cases auto-suggestion should be in harmony with the wish. For example, if verbal suggestion is used, it should be affirmative, the phrase 'I shall be calm' being preferable to 'I shall not be nervous'—a suggestion that will bring negative results.

Anything in the way of a conscious command may so antagonize the inner mind that it may become temporarily unmanageable; effectual suggestion, like modern advertising, is subtle and persuasive. When communing with himself, therefore, the extremely nervous performer should say, 'In time I shall enjoy playing', because more probable than 'I shall enjoy playing'—a thought for the less nervous. A possibility is acceptable to the inner mind; with an impossible suggestion it will have nothing to do.

10. *Character and Habit*

It will now be understood that though nervousness is curable, it cannot be cured overnight. Nervousness has always a cause, and behind the common form, musical stumbling, for example, can be discovered other bad habits—daily habits of hesitation. Even to postpone a letter that ought to be written may affect a musician's memory, because to hesitate weakens character; and one who habitually runs away from small difficulties may eventually feel incapable of facing the public. To be able to control one's thoughts on the platform, one must begin at home, where concentration may be practised at any moment. Merely to listen to what others say, quietly, without interrupting, is a valuable form of discipline—an exercise much neglected.

The musical performer, unlike the poet, cannot always choose his best moments for work: accepting an engagement a year ahead, he has to perform on that day, whether or not he feels in the mood. This calls for a suppleness of mind, a power to focus attention upon whatever is present, which can only be developed through years of daily practice.

In the eye of great conductors there is a straight, searching look. After commanding the attention of others for long hours at a stretch, day after day, year in, year out. they become capable of turning their mind to any one or anything with a force that can be felt. In contrast is a type of amateur who believes it possible to achieve everything the 'professional' does without taking any of the necessary pains; but if these music-lovers were obliged to attend a three-hour orchestral rehearsal, they would learn that in order to be an artist it is necessary to practise mental discipline as much as music.

There are other amateurs, however, who long to educate themselves; among them many older people who have been at the mercy of family or circumstance, and who, when at last finding themselves free for regular study, hardly know where to begin. For these self-discipline should not be too strict: it will be enough to plan out the practice hour; and, little by little, discipline can be tightened until each hour has its allotted task or relaxation. Only the trifler finds no time; the busiest can always 'make' it out of the odd five minutes here and there that others consider too short to be valuable.

11. *What is Luck?*

Success depends on so many things, but to get into a habit of considering the luck of certain days is to expect failure at stated intervals. Even if luck is affected by numbers, as some believe, a professional musician is rarely privileged to choose his concert dates.

Although memory depends on associations, all are not helpful, as was proved by a singer who had formed a habit of practising with her eyes fixed on a special picture on her studio wall. In the examination room she raised her eyes as usual, but seeing nothing but a blank wall, she broke down completely.

Pianists can be put out by an instrument other than their own. Difference of touch sometimes accounts for this, but not always: a piano sounds different in a hall, and a full grand with raised lid looks forbidding to a student used to an upright. Visual memory (along with all the others) may be upset merely by the syncoped movement of dampers usually concealed; and to such things a performer must accustom himself if he wishes his concert to be successful. Nothing should be left to luck. A stool that wobbles can be just as upsetting to memory as a note out of tune; and playing can be ruined by a chair too high or too low, which interferes with habits of technique. Lighting is important: it is just as distracting to play with a shadow across the keyboard as with a light in one's eyes. Everything should be seen to, in good time, including the heating of the artists' room; because to sit in a chilly room before a concert is enough to make any one nervous. Forethought given to matters such as these is more important than the avoidance of a ladder on the way to the concert.

Colour unconsciously affects the musician's nerves, and the decoration of a practice room is important. Brown is depressing; dark red is irritating; while some colours, including blue, are calming to the mind.

A Word to Women. High heels should not be worn on the platform: they hamper a pianist's use of the pedal, and they alter the natural balance of the body of those who perform standing. Dress is important from every point of view; but it should be chosen with an eye to comfort, the ideal being one so comfortable that the wearer does not have to think about it.

12. *Appearance*

No soloist should be in a hurry to go on or off the platform. To learn how not to walk, one has but to watch other people, most of whom bend, throwing their weight forward. On the contrary, one should walk easily, as Eastern people do, putting the weight first on the heel of the foot. This makes the body upright. (The chin should be held up, not back.) Good carriage means more than dignified appearance—it makes for deeper breathing with better health, and out of good health grows self-confidence.

13. *The Broadcaster*

Before a first broadcast it is necessary to have a rehearsal in the studio, because, when there is a carpet (as in some studios) one has to become accustomed to the tone, which sounds disappointing after the resonance of a hall. Pianos differ in height from the ground, and if there is a carpet, the piano may have to be raised before a broadcast; otherwise, a tall player may find himself unable to use the pedal. When a musician broadcasts from memory, some one should be there with the open music; but if preferring to use the copy (as many do), he should practise with the copy. One's mental image of a music page differs in some subtle way from the real thing, and after playing a piece for some time from memory, it can be very disconcerting to play from printed notes without preparation. The right person should be present to turn pages, and also to act as audience: it is less upsetting to the tiro's nerves to play for one sympathetic friend than to imagine an audience of millions.

14. *Before a Concert*

As a concert approaches, the less a musician works on his programme the better; he should go over pieces with relaxed attention, merely to prove to himself that he knows them along with headings previously arranged. The day before a concert, pieces should be gone through once only (preferably in the morning) with no rehearsal of headings; at this stage it is inadvisable to break up the music's continuity. When a musician feels he must work, he should confine himself to exercises, or to other pieces preferably familiar.

If rest is advisable before performance, how is an unoccupied musician to pass the time? Considering the last day or two as a well-earned holiday, he should seek distraction in walk, cinema, or enthralling book—anything is preferable to nervous practice. With experience, he will be able to throw over responsibility and rest in bed with a book; with still more experience, he will be able to fall asleep to pass the time.

Dressing should be leisured, and plenty of time allowed for going to the hall. There, no disturbing element should be permitted to enter the artists' room; even best friends must be refused admittance should they bring with them thoughts of fear and discouragement: the musician who has learnt to relax will be safer with a good book for company.

The music may be taken to the green-room if this gives a soloist confidence, but he should refrain from looking at it. After all, if a programme has not been mastered by the concert night, it is then too late to learn it: the printed notes should always be used rather than risk a break-down through inadequate preparation.

15. *The Programme*

Any one inclined to be nervous should give extra preparation to the beginning of a programme; and for the first piece, pianists should choose one of 'singing' character, which will give opportunity of relaxing shoulders and arms. There is much interesting music rarely performed, and a young musician will be rewarded by leaving the beaten track; critics are usually grateful to hear something new; and to play music round which no tradition has grown gives an inexperienced interpreter less cause for anxiety about possible criticism.

If a soloist feels at his best, rest periods during the programme should be short: one who has command of the situation, like a mountain climber during ascent, should not allow himself to rest for too long.

Deep breathing brings endurance; and to take a long breath at the beginning of a difficult passage is very helpful. Many performers unconsciously breathe with the phrasing of music, but an audience, too, should be unconscious of this.

It is wise to play more broadly in a hall than in a room, and the pianist who waits for the sound to 'come back' will know by instinct how to modify tempo and pedalling, which, unlike fingering, should be adapted to surroundings. To listen has many advantages, one of them being that it helps to prevent self-consciousness, any form of which can be as dangerous as doubt. (The thought 'How well I am playing this' is almost inevitably followed by a lapse of technique or memory.) Yet some performers confess their mind wanders to such an extent, even in public, that they may be quite unconscious of pages of what they play; and these musicians have yet to learn that the secret of remembering music is, paradoxically, that of forgetting—oneself. Why dread criticism? Most members of an audience come primarily to enjoy music; therefore, a performer who has survived the ordeal of students' concerts may take it for granted he is surrounded by a friendly circle who wish him well.

16. *The Open-minded*

Those who fear their public rarely get in touch with it; however good the performance, there will be lacking the mutual sympathy that helps an artist sensitive to people as well as music. Every performer has a right to count on extra help at such a time. Has not nature provided a stimulant, adrenalin, for all great occasions? If excited, instead of cramped by fear, memories and habits will respond with a clarity and speed of thought of which they may seem incapable at rehearsal.

But because the artist's ideals rise with his development, the greatest

K

may have to go on the platform time after time, only to face inward disappointment. It is this uncertainty of what is going to happen that makes many apprehensive—not afraid of failing outwardly, but afraid of being unworthy of their task. They feel humble, only too human, and rather lonely. To many it is helpful to think of subconsciousness as something beyond themselves—something that will do the work when the time comes. 'I felt as if I were being helped,' a musician will say afterwards, as if hardly daring to believe it. 'I felt as if some one were moving my arms for me,' was the secret of a conductor who had risen to the occasion. Another gifted artist, a singer, confessed that he always sang his best when he hardly knew what he was doing; and after any inspired performance the musician's eyes alone will tell you that he has emerged from a very unusual plane of experience. In retrospect, such an experience will seem like a pleasant dream; but unlike most dreams it can become more vivid with the passing of time. This picture of success should be treasured, and round it will glow a frame of confidence through which may be regarded the mental pictures of experiences to come. After all, nervousness is just the wrong frame of mind.

But those who do not love music enough to work for it rarely find in their book of experience a complete picture of artistic success. In the creation of those dreams musicians wish to come true, it is head as much as heart that makes them possible. These two are joint artists—the head in the learning, the heart in the expression, of Music.

AFTERTHOUGHT

IF one could write down all one's experiences involving memory, the book would be so thick that no one would read it.

Memory for music cannot be shoved into a pigeon-hole of the mind, being bound up with all memory, just as memory is bound up with habits, habits with character, character with life itself—for the imaginative student, a chain of thought without end.

Using this book merely as a preface to his own book of experience, the musician will find ways of memorizing of his own, and this is as it should be. The essential is to regard memory, not as an enemy, but as a willing part of oneself. What may it not bring forth if one can but let it be?

I shut my eyes, and I see myself as a little child, sitting with my father on a hill-top. The picture is particularly vivid, because it is fixed in my mind by emotion; for has not my father told me that I am changing the shape of the world? Over the precipice I throw the pebbles, one by one, thrilled by the thought that I, so small, can alter the balance of all things.

The study of music is changing its form. One difficulty after another has been removed from the student's pathway; yet he may still come to grief through misuse of memory. If my small book can help to remove this fear of forgetting, I shall not regret the passing of the years out of the experience of which it has been written.

BOOKS QUOTED

AVELING, Francis, *Directing Mental Energy*; 1927, University of London Press, Limited.

BAUDOUIN, Charles, *Suggestion and Autosuggestion*; 1920, London, George Allen & Unwin, Limited.

BUSONI, Ferruccio, *Von der Einheit der Musik*; 1922, Berlin, Max Hesses Verlag.

GROVE, George, *A Dictionary of Music and Musicians*; 1927 (3rd edition), London, Macmillan & Co., Limited.

JAMES, William, *Talks to Teachers*; 1920, London, Longmans, Green & Co., Limited.

MATTHAY, Tobias, *Musical Interpretation*; 1912, London, Joseph Williams, Limited.

PADEREWSKI, I. J., 'My Story'; 1937, *The Saturday Evening Post*; Philadelphia, The Curtis Publishing Co.

PLAYFORD, John, *An Introduction to the Skill of Musick*; 1697 (13th edition), London, E. Jones.

SWIFT, Edgar James, *Psychology and the Day's Work*; 1918, U.S.A., Charles Scribner's Sons: 1930, London, George Allen & Unwin, Limited.

ACKNOWLEDGEMENTS

THANKS are due to the following publishers for permission to reprint quotations from copyright musical works:

Editions M. P. Belaïeff and Messrs. Boosey & Hawkes: *Scriabin*: Prelude, Op. 16, No. 3; Prelude, Op. 31, No. 1.

Edition Russe de Musique and Messrs. Boosey & Hawkes: *Prokofief*: March, Op. 3.

Oxford University Press: *Chopin*: Prelude, No. 20 (from the Oxford Original Edition of Chopin).

INDEX

Accent,
bar-line and, 26–7;
prefix to, 25, 108;
rhythm and, 29, 34.
Accompaniment,
orchestral, 40;
tone of, 34, 37;
vocal, 92, 94.
Accompanist, 94.
Actions, habitual, 12–15, 80.
Actor,
interpretation of, 23, 92;
memory of, 4, 34–5.
see also Speaker.
America, musicians in, 3, 104.
Anxiety, *see* Nervousness.
Arm weight, 65, 108, 128–9.
Artist,
concentration, 19, 125–6;
habits, 40;
interpretation, 23;
self-control, 4–5, 17;
teacher, vii.
see also Performer.
Associations,
colour, 83, 102;
necessity for conscious, 33, 76–7, 80–5, 116–17;
subconscious, 10, 80–1;
useless, 83, 126;
verbal, 25, 93.
Attention,
active, 20–1;
degrees of, 20, 24;
divided, 30, 43, 65, 68, 104;
effect on habit, 40, 44, 119–20;
and fatigue, 21–2;
necessity for, 16–18, 23–5, 73, 116–17;
passive, 15, 42–4.
see also Concentration.
Audience,
eyes of, 3, 93;
mind-wandering of, 17.
see also Public.
Aveling, Francis (quoted), 4.

Bach,
lessons, 59–60, 65–7, 70–2;
teaching of, 83;
works quoted, 65–6, 69.
Bar,
counting of, 90;
stress of, 36, 63.
Bar-lines, misplacing of, 26–7, 48, 55, 72, 76.
Bass,
importance of, 49, 64;
practice of, 69.
Baudouin (quoted), 14, 20.
Beat,
stress of, 36;
subdivision (grouping of), 26–30, 34.
see also Accent.
Beethoven,
lesson, 60–1;
works quoted, 29, 35, 37, 61–2.
Body,
balance of, 127;
mind and, 12, 42.
Boredom, 21–2, 38, 73. *See also* Fatigue.
Boult, Sir Adrian (quoted), 102.
Bowing, 28, 99.
Brahms,
lesson, 97;
work quoted, 25.
Breakdown,
cause of, 15, 18, 108, 110, 126;
experience of, 44, 120–4.
see also Failure of memory.
Breathing, 110, 127, 129. *See also* Phrasing.
Broadcasting, 25, 127–8.
Bülow, von, 2, 4, 122.
Busoni, Ferruccio (quoted), 2–3, 5.

Child, Children,
association, 83;
concentration, 19, 80–1, 84–5;
education, 19–21, 78;
memory, 18, 80, 84–5;
mind-wandering, 18–19.
see also Pupil.